LIFE AND WRITINGS OF
TOBIAS GEORGE SMOLLETT

Life and Writings

of

Tobias George Smollett

BY

DAVID HANNAY

BOOKS FOR LIBRARIES PRESS
FREEPORT, NEW YORK

First Published 1887
Reprinted 1971

INTERNATIONAL STANDARD BOOK NUMBER:
0-8369-5767-9

LIBRARY OF CONGRESS CATALOG CARD NUMBER:
74-154151

PRINTED IN THE UNITED STATES OF AMERICA

CONTENTS.

CHAPTER VII.

LIFE OF SMOLLETT.

—•—

CHAPTER I.

TOBIAS GEORGE SMOLLETT was born in 1721, the younger son of a younger son of a Scotch laird, in that part of Dumbartonshire, known as the Lennox. The exact date of his birth is unknown; but he was baptized on the 19th of March, and was doubtless born in that month. His family were gentlefolk. He was a gentleman of coat-armour, and in France would have been counted noble. The Smolletts of Bonhill belonged, however, to use the French phrase, rather to the *noblesse de robe* than to the *noblesse d'épée*. The novelist's grandfather, Sir James Smollett of Bonhill, was for part of his life a judge in the Commissary Court, and, though the family gave, like other Scotch houses, many of its younger sons to the noble profession of arms, most of its members were lawyers or men of business. The antiquity of the family was not great, but their position as gentry was so clearly recognized, that Sir James Smollett "intermarried." with a daughter of McAulay of Ardencaple, who was no less a dignitary than heritable bailie of the Lennox. He—that is Sir James—

was an active and successful man, not only as a lawyer and
laird, but as a politician, for he was sent by the burghers
of Dumbarton to several of the old Scots' Parliaments,
from 1685 onwards.   Finally, he was named one of the
commissioners for carrying through the Act of Union with
England in 1707. This event put an end to his political
career, and he spent the last years of his life in mana-
ging, and, as it would seem, adding to his patrimonial
estate of Bonhill.   Sir James was a Whig and a Pres-
byterian.   There is nothing to show that he in any way
sympathized with the wilder and fiercer sections of his
party and his Church in the bad days before the
revolution, but he may be guessed to have been a somewhat dour and hard-fisted Scot of the worldly religious
type.

Sir James so far enjoyed the blessings promised to the
just man that he had a family of children, four of them
sons, who he might hope would carry on his name and
his works.   The blessing was not however unmixed.
The eldest son Tobias, after serving in Lord Strathmore's
regiment, died young, leaving only a daughter.   The
second, James, and the third, George, who were lawyers,
do not seem to have been successful men.   James fell
into trouble and died before his father.   The old laird
must have had some ground of complaint against the
third son, George, for when he settled his estate, he left
it, firstly, to his grandson James, the son of James, and
then to his grandson James, the son of George, although
this one of his sons was alive at that time.   There is no
mention in the will of his fourth son Archibald, or of
Archibald's children, unquestionably because he had

given the old laird, what, from his point of view at least, was very reasonable cause of offence.

Archibald Smollett is said to have been of weak health; he was unable to follow any profession, which must of itself have been a sad grievance to Sir James. Scotchmen of his type, or of the type to which he may be guessed to have belonged, have very little toleration for weakness. They are a little apt to think it at least first cousin to worthlessness. Not content with being incapable of increasing the family fortune, Archibald Smollett burdened the estate with a portionless wife and three children. There is no evidence that old Sir James was particularly harsh to his son for this offence, but he must have been a very exceptional lawyer and laird if he did not feel offended. From the sentimental point of view Archibald was no doubt fully justified, but the laird would not improbably point out to him that the estate was not a matter of sentiment. He did not behave with the inhumanity shown by Roderick Random's grandfather. He did not turn his son out of doors, though he may have used strong language. He supplied his improvident son with a sufficiency calculated on a rather austere scale. Archibald was allowed to occupy a house at Dalquhurn on the family estate, with a modest pension, and with leave to make what he could out of a small farm, there to try if he could obtain those means of subsistence for his wife and family which it would have been more prudent in him to have acquired at an earlier period.

This Archibald Smollett and his wife, Barbara Cunningham, (be it remembered that the wife did not legally lose her own name in Scotland, which is a country with a legal system based on the Roman), were the parents of Tobias Smollett, the novelist, who was the youngest of their three children.

The father died soon after the boy's birth in 1721, leaving his widow and three children to subsist on the charity of the family. If this was not generous, it was at least sufficient. Old Sir James and the two Jameses who successively inherited Bonhill provided for the subsistence of Barbara Cunningham in a decent way. It would appear that she was allowed to continue to live at Dalquhurn after her husband's death. Mr. Chambers has found from the family records that, in 1735, a sum of 400 merks, that is, £22 4s. 5d., was yearly assigned for the support of Archibald Smollett's children "until they are twelve years old." This does not sound much, but it was a larger sum in Scotland during the first half of the eighteenth century than it would be now. It was, in fact, precisely half the jointure secured to the widow of old Sir James, and was probably thought to be an ample provision for three children, who ought never to have plagued the family by their existence. Archibald's widow would doubtless be left to make what she could out of the fields round Dalquhurn. The children were possibly brought up on a little oatmeal, but their youth would not therefore be harder than that of many hundreds of Scotch children of equally good birth in those times. With a house, a small sum of ready money, a field to keep a cow and the command of oatmeal, a thrifty Scotchwoman would have no difficulty in bringing up her children in health, and even in giving them as much training as would fit them to make a fight for themselves in the world. Neither did the Bonhill family withdraw their help when the children were twelve years old. The eldest son, James (the frequency of this name in the Smollett kin is very confusing), received a commission in the army, no doubt by the family influence. He rose to the command of a company, and is said to have gained the character of a good officer, when he was drowned at sea in the shipwreck of a transport, off the coast of America. The second child, a daughter named Jane, was so far recognized by the Smolletts that she was able to make a fairly good marriage. She became the wife of one Mr. Telfer, a successful man of business.

Tobias was provided for in a more peaceful profession than his elder brother. After preliminary schooling at Dumbarton, under Mr. John Love, of whom it is said that he was noted for his knowledge of Latin, Tobias was apprenticed to a Mr. John Gordon, described as a medical practitioner, which meant at that time both apothecary and doctor, in Glasgow. Here he remained until 1739 It would be quite in keeping with past and present Scotch custom, if Smollett varied his work for Mr. John Gordon by attending the courses at the University of Glasgow. At least it is a sufficiently safe guess that he did so, for he possessed a knowledge of Latin and even of Greek, which is hardly consistent with the supposition that he was kept strictly to Mr. John Gordon's shop. Certainly he found time to write a tragedy in five acts—no great task, it is true, for the ambition of youth—before he was eighteen. In 1739, he started for London on his adventures, fortified with some general information, a certain knowledge of medicine, a light purse, a bundle of letters of recommendation from his family, and the manuscript of his tragedy in his pocket.

These are the dry facts of Smollett's youth. How far they ought to be read and interpreted with the help of his romances is very doubtful. There is much in the early part of " Roderick Random " which has somewhat the look of autobiography. If Smollett's first story is to be treated as an authority for his life, then it must be accepted as a fact that his youth was singularly unhappy. But "Roderick Random " can only be accepted as autobiography with many reservations. The hero is, it is true, the offspring of an injudicious love match, he is an orphan, brought up by the grudging charity of kinsfolk, he is an apothecary's apprentice, and finally, he, too, departs along "the finest prospect a Scotchman ever sees," the great North Road which leads to London. Smollett had the same experience, but with a difference. The brutality, of which there is too much in "Roderick Random," begins with the boy's life ; his grandfather, his uncles and aunts, his schoolfellows are all banded to persecute him; his only protections beyond the precarious help of Lieutenant Bowling are his own fierce courage and his ingenuity in repaying evil with evil. Smollett's youth was happier than that. He was not without other protectors, and the help given him was at least sufficient. Still "Roderick Random " may be taken as an authority, in this sense, that if it gives no true picture of what actually happened to Smollett, it is a

very fair statement of what he was inclined to think
had befallen him. When Dr. Swift was reproached
with ingratitude to the uncle who had given him his
education, he replied, "he gave me the education of
a dog." Smollett had, all through his life, a sufficiently
high estimate of what was due to himself to make it
highly probable that at least during his early years he
was inclined to take the same grudging view of his
kinsmen's benefactions. He certainly, if his novels are
to be trusted as expressing his opinions, thought that
his father had had hard measure. In several of his
stories, beginning with "Roderick Random," he introduces a son or daughter, who has made an unworldly
marriage against the will of a coldly prudent parent.
In every case it is with manifest sympathy for the young
people, a very hearty detestation for the stern parent.
According to the morality of his novels, the ardent lover
has a natural right to draw freely on the paternal purse.
On sentimental principles this is perfectly sound, and
the novelist is entitled to say that his hero's desire to
possess his mistress is more to be regarded than the
wish of the hero's father to guard the contents of his
purse. It is probable, however, that Smollett would
not have made so repeated a use of this commonplace
of romance if he had not had the memory of his father's
marriage, to give it a certain personal interest to himself.
When he first began to draw a picture of whatever men
do, he naturally used up his own experience, and his
early life by the banks of the Leven or in Glasgow
would be used together with his service in the navy. It
is part of the critic's task to try and settle how far

Smollett's interpretation of life is to be accepted as the work of the cool observer, how far it is consciously and deliberately exaggerated for artistic purposes, and how far it was coloured by his own temperament. This work will be more appropriately attempted when we come to "Roderick Random."

The few stories—indeed the two stories—of Smollett's youth which are reported on tolerable evidence are neither very instructive nor very edifying. It is said in a general way that he was fond of satire. This rather stately phrase may be taken to mean that he had a boyish habit of saying things which he knew would be disagreeable to other people, and some skill in pointing his ill-nature at the obvious defects of those he chose to attack. Smollett, in common with many of the eighteenth-century writers even less qualified for the place of censor of morals, began early to lash the vices of the age. It was a common practice during a great part of the eighteenth century; and it is probable enough that the first sinners whom Smollett thought fit to reprove were his cousins, his masters and pastors, and all such persons as thought they were set in authority over him by birth or age. No specimen of this juvenile domestic satire is preserved. The two stories actually recorded are unhappily a little dull. Sir Walter Scott had heard that his master, Mr. John Gordon, expressed a preference for " my ain bubbly-nosed callant with the stane in his pouch," over the more orderly apprentices of his friends. As Sir Walter interprets this unpleasant description, it means that Smollett was a somewhat dirty boy of spirit and re-source. An ill-natured commentator might say that the description continued to be true of him till the end, but Smollett must have had kindliness enough to secure the good opinion of his master. The other story is preserved by Dr. John Moore, commonly described as the ingenious author of " Zeluco." · It is as follows :—

" On a winter evening, when the streets were covered with snow, Smollett happened to be engaged in a snowball fight with a few boys of his own age. Among his associates was the apprentice of that surgeon who is supposed to have been delineated under the name of Crab in 'Roderick. Random.' He entered his shop while his apprentice was in the heat of the engagement. On the return of the latter the master remonstrated severely with him for his negligence in quitting the shop. The youth excused himself by saying that while he was employed in making up a prescription a fellow had hit him with a snow-ball, and that he had been in pursuit of the delinquent.

" 'A mighty probable story, truly,' said the master, in an ironical tone. 'I wonder how long I should stand here before it would enter into any mortal's head to throw a snowball at me?' While he was holding his head erect, with a most scornful air, he received a very severe blow in the face by a snowball.

"Smollett, who stood concealed behind the pillar at the shop-door, had heard the dialogue, and perceiving that his companion was puzzled for an answer, he extricated him by a repartee equally smart and *apropos.*"

The story might be and probably has been told of

many idle apprentices, but, such as it is, it may be accepted as the most characteristic thing known of Smollett's youth. It fits in fairly well with the tradition reported by Campbell, "that Smollett was a restive apprentice and a mischievous stripling." Doubtless he was ill enough at home in the small money-hunting business world of Glasgow. He wanted something better, or at least larger and different, and it is nowise incredible that he revenged himself for the inconveniences of his position by that "continued string of epigrammatic sarcasm" against neighbouring bores which, according to Mr. Colquhoun of Camstraddan, adorned his conversation, and for which, in that gentleman's opinion, "no talents could compensate." The victims would unquestionably agree with Mr. Colquhoun, but, unfortunately, we have no means of knowing whether these sarcasms were endowed with that amount of talent which, in the opinion of Prince Posterity, compensates for any degree of ill-nature by supplying him with amusement.

CHAPTER II.

IN 1739 Smollett was free from any family ties which could have kept him in Scotland. His brother was in the army, his sister was married, and his mother appears to have been left in possession of the house of Dalquhurn for her life, with some money allowance from her husband's family. Smollett could in any case do little towards her support by staying in Glasgow. In the natural course of things for a young Scotchman, he went to seek his fortune in England. He was not ill provided with the means of getting on. His family had still a parliamentary connection. They no longer supplied members to the House, but they were influential constituents. A letter from the head of the family to his member was a good recommendation, and Tobias was supplied with the necessary introduction to a gentleman who would be able to help him, and no doubt willing to do so when the applicant was both member of a family which could be useful at a general election, and a brother Scot. Probably the poor relation of the laird of Bonhill considered the member of Parliament as a second string to his bow. The first was the great tragedy he carried in his pocket. This work of literature was destined to cause him much ill-temper, and much of the suffering which ill-temper entails. In his "Travels through France and Italy" Smollett devotes two long pages to a Latin diagnosis of his state of health, addressed to a certain Professor F——, at Montpellier, to whom he applied in vain for medical help. In the course of this very astounding account of his sufferings, he observes in Latin, "*Systema nervosum maxime irritabile*," and the description was applicable long before his later years of chronic ill-health. In 1739 he was already very irritable, and he put himself to a very severe test when he launched on the career of unsuccessful dramatist.

The dishonesty of patrons, the unwisdom of friendly critics, the mendacity of managers, were all revealed to Smollett by this unhappy play, and he told them all to the public in the prefaces to the tragedy, and in a long episode of "Roderick Random." The proud author of "The Regicide"—this is the name of the great tragedy —obtained an introduction to Lyttelton, a known patron of literature, probably by the help of Mallet his secretary, the "beggarly Scotchman" to whom Bolingbroke left the blunderbuss he had loaded and primed against the Christian religion. We have Smollett's own evidence that he conceived great hopes of the good things he was to receive through Lyttelton's patronage. But, alas! no patron of letters can induce the hard-hearted manager to take plays which will not act. The patron seems to have put in a good word for Smollett with Garrick and other great men in the theatrical world. It was to no effect. The play never struggled onto the stage. The utmost success Smollett ever attained in connection with this piece was one of those vague promises from the manager which are only a good-natured way of telling the new playwright that his piece is unacceptable. The preface which Smollett put to the play when it was printed is lamentable reading. The vanity of a young author never produced anything more comic than this production. "Little fellows, who are sometimes called great men," "mere Goths," with "their pride and petulance," and other terms of abuse are lavished on the patrons, friends, or actors who had even the most indirect connection with this unlucky piece. Towards Lyttelton Smollett seems to have cherished a particular hostility. He ridiculed his grief at his wife's death ; and it was not until he found himself weighing the merits of his contemporaries in the grave character of historian that he pardoned the patron who failed to give " The Regicide " a chance—indeed, it was hardly more than a chance—of being damned. Towards Garrick, Smollett's feelings were equally hostile, until he was mollified by certain pecuniary transactions, and an instance of the great actor's partly genuine and partly calculated generosity.

The " Regicide " has received scanty attention from the biographers of Smollett. A crude and boyish pro-duction is the epitaph put over it, and then it is let alone. Unquestionably it deserves both these adjectives, and yet it is not uninteresting to know what the boyish work of a man who was to do work for all time, was like. Much need not be said of it, for it was a beginning which had no after consequences in Smollett's literary life, but yet it was characteristic of its author in a way. This unsuccess-ful attempt to enter on the greatest of all the fields of literature, the poetic drama, was very imitative, and it was not in the least national. That a boy of eighteen should have shown no great originality is almost a matter of course, but Smollett's hearty and unhesitating imitation was in keeping with the uniform practice of his life. When he had accumulated experience enough to justify the confidence in which he was not naturally deficient, he could put his own mark on other men's novels, but he never created one for himself, or developed an old one into a new He began, when at last he had found his path, with Le Sage, and he ended, when he was most original, with something which was assuredly Smollett, but was also Richardson, Fielding, and Sterne. The want of nationality in his 'prentice work was a feature it had in common with the writing of all eighteenth-century Scotchmen except the song writers; but it is rather more conspicuous in his case, because the particular regicide he strove to bring on the stage was the murder of the Scotch James I. at Perth. With a subject from Scotch history to work on, it is natural to expect that a young Scotchman would have put in something smacking of his race and country. The story is a terribly dramatic one. Rich as Scottish history is in tragedy and murder, it contains nothing more dreadful than the slaughter of the poet king. The journey to the north in defiance of the wise woman's warning, the free, unguarded life of James among the burghers of Perth, the cold-blooded treason of the servants who removed the bars on the convent doors, the midnight attack of the assassins, the wild scene in the Queen's chamber, the heroic self-sacrifice of Katherine Douglas, the desperate struggle of the unarmed king—

make a story fit for the Sagas. We can imagine what a would-be dramatist, writing after Victor Hugo's battle of "Hernani," would have made of it all. But Smollett lived long before that great victory, and in the eighteenth century, which was so sensible in both senses of the word. He would doubtless have described the historic story as too Gothic for his civilized time. The murder is transacted behind the scenes, James I. becomes *un roi quelconque,* any kind you please; Katherine Douglas is as if she had never lived, or thrust her arm through the staples of the queen's chamber; her place is taken by the shadowy Eleonora; Angus, Dunbar, Grime, Athol, Cattan—names full of picturesque meaning—become mere shadows who cross the stage spouting blank verse. Everything is on a great scale—big armies, big passions, and big words abound. All the killing is not done behind the scenes. "It is not good," says the wicked Cattan to the noble Angus—

> " It is not good
> To venture forth unarmed.   Courageous thane
> Receive this dagger.
> [*Attempts to stab Angus, who wrests the dagger from him and kills him.*]
> Ang.   Ha, perfidious slave !
> What means this base attempt ?   Thou shalt not 'scape.
> Cat.   Curse on my feeble arm that fail'd to strike
> The poniard to thy heart !   How like a dog
> I tamely fall despis'd !
> Ang.   Fell ruffian ! say
> Who set thee on ?   This treachery I fear
> Is but the prelude to some dreadful scene !
> Cat.   Just are thy terrors.   By th' infernal gulf
> That opens to receive me !   I would plunge

Into the abyss with joy could the success
Of Athol feast my sense !
  [*A noise of slashing swords and shrieks.*]
                    Ha ! now the sword
Of slaughter smokes ! Th' exulting thane surveys
Th' imperial scene ; while grimly smiling Grime
With purple honour deck'd——
Ang.   Tremendous powers !
Cat. O'er the fall'n tyrant strides (*dies*)."

Hereupon enters Dunbar, a virtuous youth, wounded,
who addresses the eloquent Angus as follows :—

  " I sought thee, noble thane, while yet my limbs
    Obey their lord.   I sought thee to unfold
    My zealous soul, ere yet she takes her flight.
    Stretch'd on the ground, these eyes beheld the king
    Transfix'd a lifeless corse ! and saw this arm
    Too late to save—too feeble to avenge him.
Ang.   Weep, Caledonia, weep !—thy peace is slain—
    Thy father and thy king ! O ! this event
    Like a vast mountain loads my stagg'ring soul
    And crushes all her pow'rs.   But say, my friend,
    If yet thy strength permits, how this befell."

Dunbar does so at some length, until enter Eleonora,
"supported and wounded." Then they two sing their
swan song in blank verse and exchange vows and senti-
ments all of the greatest propriety. When their differences, which were serious in the first act, are cleared up,
Eleonora exclaims :—

              " Celestial powers,
Protect my father, show'r upon his——Oh ! (*dies*)."

Then Dunbar, severely correct to the last, kisses, " this

pale deserted temple of my joy," with the observation, that " chastity " will not refuse this privilege, and takes leave of life with a not unbecoming imitation of his mistress :—

> " O Eleonora ! as my flowing blood
> Is mix'd with thine—so may our mingling souls
> To bliss supernal wing our happy——Oh ! (*dies*)."

It will be seen that, judged as poetic dramatic dialogue, this is not of a high order. Historic truth is also not its note. What would have been the feelings of an Earl of Angus on being addressed as thane ? Why Bell the Cat cut down Spens of Kilspendie on a smaller provocation ! Still " The Regicide," though the work of a boyish imitator, shows some vehemence of slash in its imitation. It was further what playwriting has not always been, an honest attempt to be literature. There is too much oh ! and hah ! too many "infernal abysses " and "grisly kings;" the personages and passions are all of the stock kind, and, in short, it is very poor work, and no play at all, but it was manifestly inspired by real admiration of something which had life in its time. What value it has is purely biographical, but in that respect it is not unimportant. It shows at least that Smollett was early resolved to be a writer, and to do the best work in literature if trying would help him.

Before " The Regicide " had sunk decisively, from the dignity of a play which might appear on the stage, to the depressed position of a play "for the closet," Smollett had passed through an experience which more than any

other had an influence on his life. He had served in
the famous attack on Carthagena, and had gained his
intimate knowledge of the English sailor. As it became
clear to the aspiring dramatic poet that he was not to
benefit immediately by the profits of the third night, the
profits whereof fell to the playwright by the custom of
the time, he must needs have fallen back on his medical
knowledge. In 1740 an excellent opportunity presented
itself. A great fleet was fitting out at Spithead for the
West Indies, and there was pressing need of subordinate
officers and men. The long peace which followed the
conclusion of Queen Anne's wars had come to an end in
1739. After years of effort, the opposition had at last
forced Walpole's hand, and compelled him, much against
his will, to agree to hostilities with Spain. England was
about to try to force the Spaniards to cease annoying her
in America. She was just entering on the remarkable
struggle commonly called the war of Jenkins' Ear.
Smollett obtained a place as surgeon's mate in one of the
great line-of-battle ships, and sailed in October, under Sir
Chaloner Ogle, as a humble member of the expedition
which was to have ruined the Spanish power in America,
but did as a matter of fact only achieve huge failure
before Carthagena. Here again it is necessary to distinguish between Roderick Random and his creator.
The hero of that " delightful " book, as Thackeray calls
it, made his way into the navy if not in an irregular
manner, at least entirely on his own merits. Smollett
was not without friends and recommendation ; Mr.
Chambers guesses that he was helped by Sir Andrew
Mitchell, who was some time after this Secretary to the

Marquess of Tweeddale, the Minister for Scotland from
1742 to 1745, and who was more famous later on as
Minister at the Court, or rather the Camp, of Frederick
the Great during the Seven Years' War.   Mitchell was a
kinsman of the Smolletts, and would of course, after the
manner of all good Scotchmen, help one of the family.
There was no actual relationship between the novelist
and the future ambassador.   Sir Andrew Mitchell and
James Smollett, Tobias' cousin, were sisters' sons, and
what the politician did would of course be done to help
his kinsman to provide for a poor relation.   One would
be glad to know that the genial Aberdonian had a
share in putting the historian of the Carthagena expedition in the way of serving his country, but there is no
evidence that he did.   It is a mere discoursing of pro-
babilities, as Cromwell would have said, to suppose that
he exerted himself in the matter.   All we can say is that
wherever a Scotchman has influence he is likely to use it
in favour of a countryman, and particularly one who has
a family claim on him.   Not only is the exact means of
Smollett's entry into the navy unknown, but there is no
certainty as to which of the sixteen ships in Ogle's fleet
he served on.   Anderson reports that his name was
carved on the timbers of the *Cumberland*, an eighty-gun
ship, and it has been supposed that he formed part of
her crew.   He does not, however, appear on her pay-
book, and he himself in the account he wrote of the
expedition simply says that he was on board one of " the
largest ships in the fleet."

   It was on the whole Smollett's good fortune that he
saw the navy at the very lowest point it has reached since

there was a navy in England. We could wish that such
an eye-witness had been present to give an account of
som : great victory, won by Rodney or Hood, and to
draw the service at a time when its spirit was high and
its discipline was strict, without being so barbarous as it
was in the dead middle of the eighteenth century. But
though happier times would have supplied him with
materials for a nobler picture, they would hardly have
given him such extraordinary types of the old sea world
as were actually thrown in his way. In 1740 the navy
was still as little organized as it had been in the seventeenth century. It was probably even more savage.
The early half of the eighteenth century was a particularly brutal time. Along with the Hanoverian rat there
had come into England something of the callous bar-
barism produced in Germany by the Thirty Years' War,
and the sea life had been hardened along with the rest.
The assertion is hardly capable of complete proof, but
there is at least much evidence to show that there was more
flogging, and more callous cruelty in every way, at sea as
well as on shore, than there had been a century earlier.
The old isolation of the sailor's life had also been if anything increased, at least in the navy. Commissions
were longer and ships stayed much more abroad. As a
matter of course all that was peculiar or erratic in any
man's character was exaggerated by the separation from
life on shore. The whole body were, as they then
always had been, and have to some extent continued to
be, a nation by themselves. A few years later the great
moral change which passed over England in the latter
half of the eighteenth century, had begun to affect that

part of it which lived on the sea. But in 1740 the old world was still there unchanged and unsoftened.

At that time, too, the relaxation of discipline in the higher ranks, the lowering of the standard of conduct and manners in the public service, the rancour of party spirit which had coincided with, if they were not the consequences of, Walpole's administration, had all affected the navy. There was a kind of outbreak of men's passions, and a reckless subordination of duty to personal spite or personal interest, which I think it would be hard to parallel at any other time. Our priceless parliamentary institutions had their own by no means insignificant influence in producing or aggravating these evils. Admirals were Members of Parliament or at least members of a party; they were Ministerialists or Patriots first, and naval officers afterwards. With the captains it was much the same. Both looked to intrigue or interest, and not to good service, to secure them promotion. The English navy has never wanted for brave and honourable officers, and even the political seamen were not necessarily destitute of parts or courage. Vernon would fight the Spaniards as heartily as he abused Walpole. But fighting the Spaniards was not his sole, nor always his first, object. He had his parliamentary battle to conduct at sea as well as on shore. As it was with him, so it was with other men, and hence came the endless wrangles and many of the derelictions of duty which disgraced the navy during the war of Jenkins' Ear. In any case men who had such an example set them were very likely to be slack in the discharge of their duty. It required a great explosion of national wrath and the sacrifice of an

offender who was not worse than many others to restore
the tone of the service.

These admirals and these captains might be bad
officers, but in one sense of the word they were thorough
seamen.   They had the rudeness and want of self-
restraint developed in them by their solitary life and
the exercise of almost unchecked authority.   They were
not only brutal, but proud of their brutality.   They
might help the landsman in his political intrigues, but
they despised him.   In particular they despised and hated
the soldier.   On active service they gave a full swing to
their hatreds and prejudices, and even exaggerated them
out of mere ostentation.   The men who obeyed their
orders were a race apart like themselves, though less
affected by the influences which had to a large extent cor-
rupted the officers of that generation.   They were always
ready to follow bravely where they were bravely led, sub-
mitting without a murmur, and even as a matter of course,
to a ferocity of treatment unparalleled in these times
even in a Russian prison, and with a language, with
loves, hates, prejudices, and superstitions all their own.
Then too the navy was not fully at that time a service
in the modern sense.   It did not stand apart from the
wilder or even the more criminal elements of the sea life.
Officers and men passed from the navy to the merchant
service (and in those days merchant seaman and armed
smuggler were very commonly convertible terms, at least
on the coast of Spanish America) and back again.   There
were even cases in which men who had gone far beyond
armed smuggling were found serving King George, and
that not always before the mast.   All was fish that came

to the press-gang's net. Smugglers, pirates, poachers, burglars, highwaymen, and insolvent debtors were allowed to volunteer on board the fleet, there to serve by the side of real seamen, and under the orders of officers sometimes of doubtful antecedents and too often inclined to rule by terror. In this very expedition to Carthagena, Admiral Vernon had no scruple about giving a lieutenant's commission to a seaman possessed of an accurate know ledge of the Spanish Main which he had acquired in a way sufficiently indicated by his name and designation —Lowther the Pirate.

No doubt there were men of honour, at once gentle men and seamen, in his Majesty's service. Anson, Sir Chaloner Ogle, and such officers as the Lord Aubrey Beauclerc, who died on the deck of his ship, the *Prince Frederick*, at Carthagena, were there, with inferior men. Under them were subordinate officers, not inferior to themselves in quality. There were seamen before the mast no less brave, loyal, and skilful than the crews of Drake or of Nelson. Happily, England has never yet wanted for such men, and in that bad year of the middle of the eighteenth century there were enough of them to fight England through to final victory. After some twenty years of warfare, and with the help of vehement public support, they were able to conquer the bad element, and to begin the formation of that magnificent fleet of the Great War, which saved England, and through her saved Europe. But in 1740 the bad element was at its very worst, and was, moreover, in power. With the single ex ception of Anson's great voyage, the navy did nothing worthy of its predecessor of the seventeenth century, or its

3

successor of the great war, during the war of Jenkins' Ear. It was very barbarous, full of a rude courage, and a real seamanship ; but it was undisciplined, badly led, and deficient in zeal. All that was worst and wildest in it broke loose under such leadership as was inflicted on it. This was the navy which Smollett saw and which he drew.

It would be out of place to give the history of the attack on Carthagena in a life of Tobias Smollett. He has himself told the story twice over, or rather thrice ;— in his history he has told it briefly in its place ; he wrote a special account of it for the series of voyages he edited as part of the vast miscellaneous hack-work of his later literary life ; and it has its very conspicuous share in making the interest of "Roderick Random." It was a scene which must have impressed him profoundly. The abundant courage displayed in carrying one after another of the Spanish defences, as far as the San Lazaro, the ready devotion of soldiers and sailors alike, were calculated to win the hearty sympathy of a man who had his full share of the old Scotch pugnacity. Individual episodes, such as the gallantry of Lord Aubrey Beauclerc, would move him deeply. But there was another side which manifestly made a more lasting impression upon him. The misconduct, the insolent, heartless cruelty of Vernon, the stupid professional pedantry and ignorance of General Wentworth, the lamentable delays, the wrangling, the dishonest make-believes of too many officers of both services, fed fat his inborn scorn for human stupidity and dishonesty. He was by nature a hater of fools, and after seeing those fatal persons at work at Carthagena, he was not likely to be softer in his

judgment than before. Smollett was not a sentimental
man, but he did not love cruelty, particularly when it was
the consequence of other men's folly and roguery. There
is an honest ring of indignation in his awful picture of
the misery which the quarrels and incompetence of the
leaders brought on the brave men entrusted to their
care.

In "Roderick Random" the scene is described with
a certain deliberate exaggeration, a heightening of the
colour for artistic effect. The "Account of the Expedition against Carthagena" gives his sober and mature
view of the transaction. Two passages may be quoted
here to put Smollett's experience before the reader in
Smollett's words. The first shows the leaders at work :

"It is a melancholy truth, which, however, ought to be
told, that a low, ridiculous, and pernicious jealousy sub-
sisted between the land and sea officers during this whole
expedition, and that the chiefs of these were so weak or
wicked as to take all opportunities of thwarting and
manifesting their contempt for each other, at a time
when the lives of so many brave fellow-subjects were at
stake, and when the interest and honour of their country
required the utmost zeal and unanimity. Instead of con-
ferring personally, and co-operating with vigour and
cordiality, they began to hold separate councils, drew up
acrimonious remonstrances, and sent irritating messages
to each other ; and while each of them piqued himself
upon doing barely as much as would screen him from
the censure of a court-martial, neither seemed displeased
at the neglect of his colleague, but, on the contrary, both

were in appearance glad of the miscarriage of the expedition, in hope of seeing one another stigmatized with infamy and disgrace. In a word, the Admiral was a man of weak understanding, strong prejudices, boundless arrogance, and overboiling passions; and the General, though he had some parts, was wholly defective in point of experience, confidence, and resolution."

So much for the leadership. As Smollett saw it, it was worse than the co-operation recorded by Marryat, when the General damned the Admiral for not knocking down walls thirty feet thick, and the Admiral was equally emphatic with the General for not scaling walls thirty feet high. The consequences are told a few paragraphs further on:—

"It was, therefore, found necessary to effect a retreat, which was secured by means of those five hundred men who brought up the rear ; but not before the loss of the English amounted to two hundred killed, and twice that number wounded, of which last the majority did not recover. Sixteen of these were taken prisoners by the Spaniards, who treated them with great humanity, and loudly extolled the valour of the assailants; and a cessation of arms was immediately agreed upon for a few hours, during which time the dead were buried. Meanwhile a breastwork was raised at the advanced guard, to put the men under cover, and the intrenchment enlarged for the reception of two mortars, which in two days began to fire upon San Lazaro with good effect.

"As for the sick and wounded, they were next day

sent on board the transports and vessels called hospital
ships, where they languished in want of every necessary
comfort and accommodation. They were destitute of
surgeons, nurses, cooks, and proper provision ; they were
pent up between decks in small vessels, where they had
not room to sit upright ; they wallowed in filth, myriads
of maggots were hatched in the putrefaction of their
sores, which had no other dressing than that of being
washed by themselves with their own allowance of
brandy ; and nothing was heard but groans, lamentations,
and the language of despair, invoking death to deliver
them from their miseries. What served to encourage
this despondence was the prospect of those poor wretches
who had strength and opportunity to look around them,
for there they beheld the naked bodies of their fellow-
soldiers and comrades floating up and down the harbour,
affording prey to the carrion crows and sharks, which
tore them in pieces without interruption, and contributing
by their stench to the mortality that prevailed.

"This picture cannot fail to be shocking to the humane
reader, especially when he is informed that while these
miserable objects cried in vain for assistance, and actually
perished for want of proper attendance, every ship of
war in the fleet could have spared a couple of surgeons
for their relief, and many young gentlemen of that profession solicited their captains in vain for leave to go and
administer help to the sick and wounded. The neces-
sities of the poor people were well known, the remedy
was easy and apparent; but the discord between the chiefs
was inflamed to such a degree of diabolical rancour that
the one chose rather to see his men perish than to ask

help of the other, who disdained to offer his assistance
unasked, though it might have saved the lives of his
fellow-subjects."

It is a dreadful picture, but there is no reason to
suppose that it is overdrawn. Smollett may have deliberately exaggerated in his novels, but here his quiet style
and independent evidence go to show that he was telling
the strict disgraceful truth. By bringing it home to his
countrymen Smollett did the State no small service.
"Roderick Random," and this account, enabled thousands of Englishmen to realize the consequences of such
conduct as Vernon's and Wentworth's. He did, in fact,
with even better justification, and, I trust it may be said
without offence, in a better literary form, what the correspondents of newspapers did during the Crimean war.
He helped to make his generation understand what a
hatefully cruel thing military inefficiency is, and how
surely the wretched personal squabbles of leaders mean
death and useless suffering to the men who are so unhappy as to be placed at their mercy. It is, I hope, not
very ferocious to think with some complacency that
Smollett unwittingly, but not the less beneficially, helped
to prepare the people of England to insist on the execution
of Admiral Byng, and to give all leaders in war an un-
forgetable warning that their personal feelings were not
to come in the way of the discharge of their duty. Even
if he did not influence the mind of his generation in this
way, he did a considerable feat when he gave the best
literary picture of a military expedition left by any eye-
witness in the eighteenth century. Carlyle, with his

usual love of good literature and good intellectual eye-sight, and in his own emphatic way, has declared that almost the only noticeable feature in the whole expedition was the presence of Tobias Smollett. This much at least is certain, that without Tobias Smollett the Carthagena expedition would be a much less conspicuous event than it is. It would have been an ordinary defeat. Thanks to him it became a warning, and so helped to prevent the recurrence of anything quite so disgraceful in after times. Admirals and Generals quarrelled and bungled, but at least they took some pains to avoid being as Vernon and Wentworth.

CHAPTER III.

FROM Carthagena Vernon's unfortunate fleet returned to Jamaica, utterly crippled by the malarious fever which had attacked it during the siege. It fell into a miserable impotent welter, and there remained. Smollett, whose mission, says Carlyle, was "to take Portraiture of English Seamanhood with due grimness, due fidelity, and convey the same to remote generations, before it vanished," had got all he needed from his service in the fleet. Even if he was not disgusted with the mere hardships of the life, there can have been nothing in the prospects before him as a surgeon's mate to tempt him to remain at sea. It was some years before he definitely gave up all attempts to make a living as a doctor, but, even in the West Indies, he could find more pleasant and more profitable places to try in than the cockpit of a man-of-war. Very soon, apparently, after the return of the defeated expedition, he retired from service and settled for a time in Jamaica.

His stay in this sugar island was short, and left curiously little trace in his work. The society of planters and adventurers does not seem to have impressed him at all, otherwise he would surely have found room for some West Indian personage by the side of Pipes and Hatch-

way. He left the field untouched and free for the author
of "Tom Cringle's Log" and the "Cruise of the *Midge.*"
In his life the stay in the West Indies had a very important part, not to say the most important and beneficent.
He found a wife in Jamaica. The biographer, however
good his will may be, cannot say much of Mrs. Smollett.
That her maiden name was Anne Lascelles (Smollett himself calls her "Miss Nancy Lassells"), that she possessed
some property in Kingston, partly in houses and partly in
slaves, which melted away in lawsuits, and that she survived her husband for several years, is all that is known
about her. The information as to her character is even
more scanty. It is said that she was the original of Narcissa
in "Roderick Random," but as nobody has ever yet succeeded in associating any kind of human reality with the
name of that spotless heroine, this statement does not
lead us much further. If Mrs. Smollett sat for the portrait of the lady who crowned Roderick's flame, she must
be supposed to have been tall, to have had a beautiful
figure and a fine head of black hair. These things can
be asserted of Narcissa, and that is nearly all. It is even
doubtful whether the marriage took place in Jamaica or
later on in London. Mr. and Mrs. Smollett do not seem
to have begun living together in England until 1747, but
it is probable that Smollett was in possession of his wife
and her fortune before he left Jamaica in 1744. Between
his arrival in London about that time and the appearance
of "Roderick Random" in 1748, Smollett, as far as his
own exertions are concerned, came as near as possible to
being without visible means of subsistence. He may, of
course, have got possession of a slice of prize-money in

the West Indies. Pleasant little sums of money were
picked up by naval gentlemen in irregular ways. He may
have earned something in Jamaica, but there is no evidence that he got anything beyond his scanty pay as
surgeon's mate. In London he certainly cannot have
made enough to live on. Medical practice he never
obtained, and his literary gain must have been insignificant before the publication of his first novel. Yet he was
not without means. By the summer of 1744 he had
rented a house in Downing Street, Westminster. He
writes in May to his friend Barclay in Glasgow, informing
him that, " I have moved into the house where the late
John Douglas, surgeon, died, and you may henceforth
direct for Mr. Smollett, Surgeon in Downing Street,
Westminster." Houses in Downing Street, Westminster,
are not to be obtained without payment of rent, and
Smollett must have found the money somewhere. Neither
was he without funds for other and less serious purposes.
In this very letter, which begins with a lament over a
friend of the name of Ritchie, he ends briskly by saying
that Willie Wood is drinking a glass of wine with him,
presumably at Smollett's own expense. A passage in this
letter may be quoted as a proof that he was already
married. "As for the particulars you expect from me you
must wait till I be better informed myself; for, to tell you
an extraordinary truth, I do not know as yet whether you
had better congratulate or condole with me. I wish I
was near you that I might pour forth my heart before you
and make you judge of its dictates and the several steps
I have lately taken, in which case I am confident you and
all honest men would acquit my principles, however my

prudentials might be condemned." This certainly sounds
like a reference to a not very wise marriage, though to be
sure it is not easy to see why "the prudentials" of a
penniless Scotch gentleman should be condemned for
marrying a West Indian heiress. On the whole, it seems
more probable that Smollett was married before coming
to London, and that he lived chiefly on his wife's money
until he began to earn a livelihood by his pen. As was
the case with other literary men of that century, Smollett's
financial resources are occasionally obscure, and he had
his periods of debt and difficulty, but he never seems to
have been absolutely without means. There was always
the wherewithal for "a glass of wine," and even for
travels of a rather costly kind.

The best, and not the least pleasant, of the scanty personal notices of Smollett is dated in the following year,
and during the exciting times of the '45. Dr. Alexander
Carlyle, deservedly called Jupiter Carlyle, whose charming
autobiography has been edited by Mr. Hill Burton, has
described the beginning of his acquaintance, for it can
hardly be said to have been friendship, with Smollett.
The future minister of Inveresk, after witnessing the battle
of Preston Pans, had come to London by way of Holland,
and there, in that pleasant military and literary society
with which he was exceptionally popular for a Presby-
terian minister, he met the future author of "Roderick
Random." Carlyle; John Blair, who afterwards took
orders in the Church of England, and became tutor to
the Duke of York and Prebendary of Westminster;
Smith, who had been tutor to the Laird of McLeod when
that youthful chieftain had the good fortune to be out of

the way on the landing of Prince Charlie at Loch Na
Nuagh, and Smollett used to meet together like good
Scotchmen at a coffee-house in Cockspur Street, and
passed pleasant evenings together. "We four," says Carlyle, "with one or two more, frequently resorted to a small
tavern in the corner of Cockspur Street at the Golden Ball,
where we had a frugal supper and a little punch, as the
finances of none of the company were in very good order.
But we had rich enough conversation on literary subjects,
which was enlivened by Smollett's agreeable stories,
which he told with peculiar grace."

Carlyle had to undergo the common fate of gentlemen
who know an unsuccessful dramatic author. He was
shown the manuscript of "James I. of Scotland," and no
doubt had to hear all the sins of the managers, but he
extricated himself from this pass with the judgment which
he frequently showed in later days, when he was a distin-
guished member of the Moderate party in the General
Assembly. As he remained on friendly terms with
Smollett, he doubtless contrived to escape without expressing an opinion on the merits of "The Regicide."
In his autobiography he seems to agree with the estimate
of the managers, and he was too honest a man to have
said what he did not think. His Scotch caution would
instruct him to stand on guard against the other man's
Scotch ardour, by not saying all he did think. A more
detailed mention of Smollett follows Dr. Carlyle's brief
dismissal of the play and its fortunes.

"I was in the coffee-house with Smollett when the news
of the Battle of Culloden arrived, and when London all
over was in a perfect uproar of joy. . . . About nine

o'clock I wished to go home to Lyon's in New Bond Street, as I had promised to sup with him that night, it being the anniversary of his marriage night, or the birthday of one of his children. I asked Smollett if he was ready to go, as he lived in May Fair; he said he was and would conduct me. The mob was so riotous, and the squibs so numerous and incessant that we were glad to go into a narrow entry to put our wigs into our pockets and to take our swords from our belts and to walk with them in our hands, as everybody then wore swords ; and after cautioning me against speaking a word lest the mob should discover my country and become insolent, 'for John Bull,' says he, 'is as haughty and valiant to-night as he was abject and cowardly on the black Wednesday when the Highlanders were at Derby.' After we got to the head of the Haymarket, through incessant fire, the doctor led me by narrow lanes, where we met nobody but a few boys at a pitiful bonfire, who very civilly asked us for sixpence, which I gave them. I saw not Smollett again for some time after, when he showed Smith and me the manuscript of his ' Tears of Scotland,' which was published not long after, and had such a run of approbation. Smollett, though a Tory, was not a Jacobite, but he had the feelings of a Scotch gentleman on the reported cruelties which were said to be exercised after the Battle of Culloden.''

Dr. Carlyle wrote his memoirs in extreme old age in the very first year of this century, some sixty years after his first meeting with Smollett, and thirty years after the novelist's death. It is possible that in speaking of Smollett as a Tory he was making a little mistake in perspective, and crediting him with political opinions, matured, according to a better authority, during his historical investigations into the rascality of the Revolution Whigs. The " Tears of Scotland" are proof enough that Dr. Carlyle was not wrong in his description of Smollett's feelings on hearing of the Battle of Culloden, and the cruelties of " Butcher" Cumberland's army. The author of "Roderick Random,"who apologized for bringing his hero from the northern parts of this United Kingdom, and was careful to give excuses for making him a Scotchman, was not likely to parade his nationality. He acted in literature on the excellent advice he gave Dr. Carlyle, and took care not to provoke the insolence of the mob by an untimely display of the Scotch accent. But between this judicious reticence and the active simulation recommended under analogous circumstances by Mr. Pickwick, there is a difference. Smollett was not the man to shout with the largest mob, and he was an ardent Scotchman though he was too really proud a man to indulge in the weakness of insisting on his nationality, to which Dr. Johnson was apt to think no Scotchman was superior. As a Lowlander who came from the Highland Border at a time when the raids of the Celtic tribes were not wholly things of the past, he certainly had no great love for the Highlanders. If Culloden had been fought between Scotchmen he might even have welcomed the victory. It was not: it was the victory of Englishmen and Germans over a part of Scotland, and was therefore odious. Smollett boldly lamented it as a disaster. The "Tears of Scotland " is a lament as if for another Battle of Flodden. The writer draws no distinction between

Highland and Lowland, Jacobite and Hanoverian. Perhaps, or even without perhaps, it revolted a man who remembered that the exiled royal line were his countrymen, to see Scotch blood spilt, the huts of Scotch peasants go up in flames, Scotchmen of all ranks die on English scaffolds to preserve a king who came from Germany. There is some want of logic in the attitude of mind of a gentleman who was not a Jacobite, and who yet was made indignant when the Jacobites suffered the consequences of their own acts. Still the feeling was eminently national and natural. Blood *is* thicker than water, and the national feeling of any Scotchman was very much stronger than his devotion to the House of Hanover, even though he were as good a Whig as Forbes of Culloden himself. Indeed, it is hard to conceive of anybody, Englishman or Scotchman, feeling what can properly be called devotion to the Hanoverian family, in the middle of the reign of George II. Then too the details of the suppression of the rebellion were sufficiently revolting. The noisy terror of London during the march of the Highlanders to Derby, followed by a reaction of even more noisy cruelty was sure to have excited the disgust of Smollett. He might well think that even if the thing had to be done, it should have been done with more humanity and regard for the dignity of the State. Many years afterwards he asks in his travels whether some remnants of old barbarity are not still to be found in a certain island, and the question must have been partly inspired by a recollection of the burnings and shootings in the Highlands, of the shambles at Carlisle, and the scaffold in London.

The well-known story told by Mr. Graham of Gartmore, on the authority of some eye-witness unnamed, is
supported as far as it is possible by the general tone of
the poem. According to this literary legend, Smollett
read the first six stanzas of his poem to a party of friends,
in a tavern, perhaps that same coffee-house in Cockspur
Street mentioned by Dr. Carlyle. They found it a little
too vehement, and would have persuaded Smollett that
he was likely to give offence in high quarters. This
prudence had the effect it was calculated to have on a
Scotchman of the pugnacious order. The indignant
poet sat down and wrote a seventh stanza asserting his
fixed intention to go on incurring the wrath of sinners in
high quarters :—

> " While the warm blood bedews my veins,
> And unimpaired remembrance reigns,
> Resentment of my country's fate
> Within my filial breast shall beat.
> And, spite of her insulting foe,
> My sympathizing verse shall flow,
> Mourn, hapless Caledonia ! mourn,
> Thy banished peace, thy laurels torn ! "

Smollett's muse habitually inspired him best when
Scotland was the subject, and in this case his indignation
at the wrongs of his native land not only made his
verses, but made them with an unquestionable vehemence
of sincerity. If the warning of his friends was ever
given it was needless. The revengeful wrath of Englishmen, even in their hardest mood, has rarely been of long
endurance, and has never long survived victory. If they

have not always rightly interpreted the hard saying, be ye angry and sin not, at least they have not let the sun go down on their wrath. The run of approbation which Dr. Carlyle says rewarded the " Tears of Scotland " was the first sign of the speedy reaction which brought all England round to agreement with Smollett. Before many years were over the " Butcher " Cumberland was bitterly taunted for his cruelties by the very mob which had lit the bonfires for Culloden. To be sure he never gave them cause to light bonfires again.

The "Tears of Scotland " were accompanied by the two poems which may be bracketed together as the sorrows of Tobias Smollett. " Advice; a Satire," and " Reproof; a Satire"; both appeared in 1746. It was doubtless a disappointment to their author that they did not meet with any remarkable run of approbation, but at this distance of time the wonder is not that few men marked them, but that they ever came to be written. Satire, which Diogenes Teufelsdröckh described as the language of the devil, is not yet dead, on a dyke-side or elsewhere. While the devil and the things of the devil continue in existence, it is safe; but "the satire," the deliberate production of a gentleman who sets himself down to rail in verse at the vices of the age, in cold blood, and of malice aforethought, is a very extinct literary form. But in 1746 it was not only alive, but even had a future. Its classical pedigree was of the best, and the English branch of the tree bore one at least of the greatest names in literature. Pope had made it almost commendable in a young man of spirit to lash the vices of the age in heroic couplets. Dryden who was in all respects less of an eighteenth-century model than his successor, had used satire, and with dreadful effect, but it was against definite parties, and in a recognizable cause. Smollett imitated the general attack of Pope, if we ought not rather to say the general attack of Swift and the form of Pope.

Substantially these two satires of Smollett do not differ from much which is and will continue to be published. There is some general scolding at the vices of the age, and a great deal of abuse of individuals. Numbers of persons discreetly indicated by capital letters and dashes, are accused of various vices. Scandalous stories, which were of course at that time the secret of Punch, are repeated, or at least referred to. All this has its counterpart in our time, and it was as respectable then as it is now, and no more. The satire as a common literary form has one advantage over the newspaper paragraph. It is at least bound to be more literary. Heroic couplets, written in imitation of Pope, must, as long as they scan, be superior to slovenly prose notes. Their author must put a certain amount of ingenuity and of the use of the file into their production. Anybody can repeat the last ill-natured story about A's quarrels with his wife, or B's dealings with somebody else's, in newspaper English ; but, if he wants to do this in verse, he must devote some amount of ingenuity to the task. Smollett was at least as ingenious as some fifty or sixty or more gentlemen who wrote heroic verse in the eighteenth century, and if that is not exalted praise, it at least is not blame. It amounts to saying that Smollett, as his own seafaring friends would have put it, toed the line. He wanted to

make his mark in literature; he took up a popular form
in his day, and tried his hand at it; the result was two
small satires of some vivacity, the work of one who was
by nature a prose writer, but who could handle a metre
which had been put within the reach of every clever
imitator by Pope. At this distance of time, however,
clever imitation is not enough to give interest to these
satires. The labourer in that rich mine the scandalous
history of the reign of George II., will find useful lines
here and there. The follies of the town, the misfortunes
of this or the other notoriety of the day, and the disgraceful success of one or another hanger-on and unscrupulous
instrument of the great, are all denounced in the proper
way. It is all done with a lofty air of moral indignation
which is now more than a little ludicrous, but was then
part of the game. Smollett put two quotations from
Juvenal before his satires, and was logically bound to
write in his tone, and attack the vices he had attacked.
If he had looked about him for an English motto, he
would have found a very fit one. He could have said
with Jaques—

> " Give me leave
> To speak my mind, and I will through and through
> Cleanse the foul body of the infected world,
> If they will patiently receive my medicine."

The offer is always open to the duke's criticism, and
the satirist must justify his work to posterity by his work-
manship, if he is to be excused for disgorging into the
general world all the " embossed sores and headed evils,"
which he has been at the trouble of collecting.

By the nature of things the wrathful poet who will deal
in satire, finds nothing fouler in this infected world than
his own wrongs and disappointments. Smollett did not
make an exception. Between the publication of "Advice,"
and the appearance of " Reproof," he had found time for
another quarrel with a manager. He had written the
libretto of an opera, to be called "Alceste," for Rich, the
manager of Covent Garden. The music was to have
been contributed by Handel, but author and manager
fell out, and the composer transferred his music to
Dryden's " Cecilia." Nothing came of this second unlucky attempt to storm the stage except four lines of
virulent abuse of poor Rich, who is denounced with far
more fervour than Cope, Hawley, or the offending
Hanoverian General at Dettingen. When a literary
gentleman fights out a private quarrel in this public way,
he ought, in the opinion of to-day, to have some hesitation about taking up a lofty moral attitude; but this is
only our view. The wit of the eighteenth century was
troubled with no such scruples. That a literary gentleman was entitled to a comfortable subsistence at the
public expense, and that he was to be treated with
deference by such inferior persons as managers or actors,
was his pleasant conviction. When these persisted in
doing their own business in their own way, he fell savagely
upon them, and did his best to give them a lesson. He
fought his fight, too, in those times, with an obviously
sincere belief that there was something highly commendable in this line of conduct. To our milder generation,
which expects a literary gentleman to make his bread and
butter with as little parade of his personality as may be,

this attitude is apt to look truculent. In the middle of the eighteenth century, it was almost a matter of course, and when Smollett came forward with two thin quartos of verse, and rebuked the time which did not recognize the poet in the proper way, he would be understood to be making a fair use of the weapons supplied him by nature. Long after his time, so naturally modest a man as Crabbe, was firmly convinced that he was entitled to support at the hands of the rulers of the State. He was angry not only for himself, but for literature, when Thurlow neglected his verses and failed to show that promptitude in helping the poet which became a Lord Chancellor. His very real gratitude to Burke was kept well on the sane side of idolatry by a quiet conviction that the great orator had honoured himself by patronizing him.

The publication of " Reproof" marks the end of Smollett's years of apprenticeship. What he had done hitherto had not returned him more than the negative service rendered to Balzac by his first ten efforts to write a novel, which, as he said, had shown him what *not* to do. Two attempts to write for the stage had been complete failures. The satires had made some little stir, enough to render it worth while to reprint them within a brief period, but in them there could be no plenty. When everybody has been denounced all round once, the public cannot be expected to listen to repetitions. It was necessary to turn to something else. By this time it must have been obvious that the something else must still be literature. Dr. Carlyle's statement that Smollett's address in 1746 was in Mayfair, shows that the Downing

Street venture must have been given up. Without a
degree, and with no London connection, a legitimate
medical practice was not to be obtained ; and even if
there had been no honesty in the way, Smollett was a
great deal too proud, quarrelsome, and scornful, for the
trade of quack, which many eighteenth-century notabili-
ties found so lucrative. There was nothing for it but
literature, even if nature had not been pushing him in
that direction.

His first struggle in London, though it had brought him
small praise, and less pudding, cannot have been useless
to Smollett. It must have gained him acquaintances, and
some familiarity with the literary world and with the
booksellers. It must have proved to him, altogether
beyond peradventure, that he could not hope to enjoy
one of those places of dignity and emolument which fell
so frequently and pleasantly in the way of the Queen
Anne men. The memory of that golden age haunted
men of letters throughout the eighteenth century, nor was
it until the triumphant success of Sir Walter Scott had
shown how amply literature could suffice for itself, and
the development of the press had supplied those who live
by the pen with an honourable means of gaining a steady
income, that they quite gave up thinking it the duty
of Government to encourage genius with pensions. No
good fortune of that kind ever fell in Smollett's way.
What direct connection he was to have with Government
was to be mere grief and pain to him, to lead to nothing
but much uncongenial work done for indifferent reward.
By 1746 his experience must have done much to clear
away any illusions he may have cherished, and to show

him that whatever he was to gain must be paid by the readers of his work.

With this situation very clearly before him, Smollett must have begun to look about for the next thing to do. He was not a man of much modesty in his estimate of himself—not what would be called a humble-minded man. Quite the reverse. To the end of his life he was plainly convinced that because he was conscious of good faculty, therefore any literary work he did was entitled to a respectful reception, and a reward to be fixed by himself. Still the failure of the " Regicide," and the even more decided disaster of the " Alceste," must have convinced him that for the time at least the stage was shut to him. The satires were an emphatic proclamation to the world that Tobias Smollett was not to be offended with impunity, but they were no sufficient resource. Without definitively renouncing either poetry or the stage, he had to turn to another among the many mansions in the House of Letters. The novel was the field which naturally and inevitably attracted him, and in this respect he was going over the course not only of many of his contemporaries, but of the literature of his century. It would be, perhaps, inaccurate, and certainly somewhat offensive to say that there has been a divorce between English literature and the English stage since the Restoration comedy died out with Farquhar. On one side at least the release *a vinculo* has never been recognized. Goldsmith and Sheridan even succeeded in re-establishing the union for a moment. None the less there has been a steady incompatibility of character which has enforced the lesser separation—not always with friendly feelings on either side. The living influences of English literature have not been dramatic. A few acting comedies, a long series of plays for the closet which, whatever other merit they may possess, want the one thing necessary—the power to keep the stage—are all that remains of the often-renewed efforts of men of letters to revive the once natural and spontaneous connection between letters and the boards. The tradition is so great, and, to take a lower but influential consideration, the reward of success is so ample, that the effort made by successive generations of writers is perfectly natural. The failure was none the less inevitable. It may be laid down as a reasonably trustworthy rule that men who find their natural field in narrative and description cannot by any possibility work at their ease for the theatre. The limitations, the mere physical limitations, of the stage, are too strict to be endurable to men accustomed to the wide elbow-room, and divine command over time and space which are the privileges of the story-teller. When he turns to the theatre his work always shows that he is thinking of something other than the effect likely to be produced by the groups, the exits, and the entrances of his characters. The actor might correct the defect if he and the man of letters would collaborate fairly ; but work in common is barely possible for these two. The actor is perhaps a little apt to think literature as superfluous as the sandwich man thought the letter H ; and the man of letters is very prone to refuse to be dictated to by a "twopenny tearmouth" as Sir Walter called no less an artist than Kean. Mutual contempt for one another's work is not favourable to collaboration. No man was ever less fitted for it than Smollett. He had miscalled Garrick and Rich as badly as his greater countryman ever did Kean. His attitude towards either of them would assuredly have been a repetition, in his earlier days at any rate, of Vernon's contemptuous treatment of Wentworth. He was to be more fruitfully employed in his library doing solid miscellaneous work for booksellers, in the intervals of contributing his very considerable share to the original prose literature of his century.

In the first month of 1748, Smollett's successful literary life began with the publication of " Roderick Random." It was to be sufficiently laborious. His stories alone make a list of respectable length judged by the standard of his time. Five stories is a small budget as compared to Sir Walter Scott's, which again looks by no means big in bulk beside the literary baggage of later men, but it was more than Fielding or Richardson left in number of volumes, though the author of "Clarissa" was and is unrivalled in the size of his individual works among English writers. Then Smollett's general work will stand comparison in point of size with any other. Translations, political satires, books of travel from his own hand are there, and with them much work done under his direction and given to the press under the protection of his name. One large task, finished in less than two years, there is, which might have been the life work of a laborious student and writer. A complete history of England in a long series of volumes stands out somewhat strangely now in the literary labours of a novelist; but it is well enough in its place on Smollett's shelf. He did it, as a piece of useful industry which the captious might call hackwork, not because nature called him to it, or his studies had prepared him, but because he was a trustworthy literary workman ready to do all reputable work for a proper consideration. It is to the credit of the booksellers and the public of the day that the consideration was by no means contemptible. With all this he did a respectable life work of journalism, helping very materially towards the present victorious position of our Sovereign Lady the Press, and ending, after ungrateful toil, disappointment and disease, with the most original, and more wonderful still, the most kindly of his works.

CHAPTER IV.

"RODERICK RANDOM" was the first in time and the first in interest of three works which Smollett published in rapid succession. It appeared in 1748. "Peregrine Pickle" followed in 1751, and "Ferdinand Count Fathom" in 1753. These three stories may most appropriately be taken together. It is sometimes not only convenient, but critical, to take an author's works one after another. But between "Roderick Random" and "Count Fathom" there was no change and no development in Smollett. He was under the same inspiration; he worked with the same aim, and his method underwent hardly any modification. It has been said that "Peregrine Pickle" and "Count Fathom" show traces of the influence of Fielding, but the supposition could hardly be proved to have a better foundation than the date of "Tom Jones," which came between Smollett's first and his second book. There is certainly a more distinct attempt to construct a plot traceable in "Count Fathom" than in "Roderick Random," and if anybody maintains that the effort would not have been made without the encouraging example of Fielding, it is impossible to prove him in the wrong. "Tom Jones" certainly came before the "Count," and may have supplied Smollett with a model, but, if so, the imitation was not happy. The superficial plot of "Count Fathom" is so mechanical, and the attempt to give coherence to his adventures is so obviously uncongenial, that, if Smollett did indeed attempt to rival the beautiful workmanlike finish of "Tom Jones," he must have greatly miscalculated his own powers. But, in truth, the differences between the first and the last of these three "adventures" is not more than may be reasonably accounted for by the author's growing familiarity with the practice of story writing. Such influence as this familiarity had may safely be neglected, in an estimate of the merits of Smollett. It is not the plot which one reads him for. To adapt Johnson's frequently quoted criticism on Richardson, if you read Smollett for the plot you would hang yourself. A better case might be made out for the proposition, that Smollett was much more influenced by Richardson himself; at least, I think that there are scenes in "Peregrine Pickle" which would not have been written by the author of "Roderick Random" if he had not read "Clarissa Harlowe" in the interval. It is almost inevitable that a writer of stories should have begun after a time to try and connect the parts by some thread of plot, but there are moral ideas and views of conduct which do not come spontaneously to all minds. When Smollett wrote his first tale he would hardly have described in the same way the scene between Peregrine and Emilia, that gross description of an attempted violation which so intensely and justly disgusted Sir Walter Scott. But whatever influence either Fielding or Richardson may have had upon him, these three books are still essentially Smollett's, and are avowedly copied from a model much older than either "Pamela" or "Tom Jones."

Smollett has saved his critics from the trouble of looking for his source of inspiration. He has named it by its name in the preface to "Roderick Random." "Of all kinds of satire," it begins, "there is none so entertaining and universally improving as that which is introduced, as it were, occasionally, in the course of an interesting story, which brings every incident home to life ; and by representing familiar scenes in an uncommon and amusing point of view, invests them with all the graces of novelty, while nature is appealed to in every particular. . . . The same method (the method of Don Quixote to wit) has been practised by other Spanish and French authors, and by none more successfully than by Monsieur Le Sage, who, in his 'Adventures of Gil Blas,' has described the knavery and foibles of life with infinite humour and sagacity. The following sheets I have modelled on his plan, taking the liberty, however, to differ from him in the execution, where I thought his particular situations were uncommon, extravagant, or peculiar to the country in which the scene is laid."

This is a sufficiently frank confession of faith. Smollett, in fact, set himself to write what in Spanish literature is called a picaresque novel, and, indeed, he went nearer the Spaniards than perhaps he was aware. Of the much which he copied from Le Sage, the spirit of Gil Blas was no part. As Smollett puts it himself, the knavery and foibles of life are the subject of the Frenchman's work. "The disgraces of Gil Blas are, for the most part, such as rather excite mirth than compassion; he himself laughs at them, and his transitions from distress to happiness, or at least ease, are so sudden, that neither the reader has time to pity him, nor himself to be acquainted with affliction." Gil Blas is thoroughly good-humoured. *L'homme moyen sensuel,* drawn by Le Sage, is a good fellow who would be honest if the world and the flesh would only let him. The personage who usually goes with these two corrupting influences does not plague Gil Blas, or at least if there is a devil in his affairs, he is not one of the great ones, but a good-natured fiend, a Devil on Two Sticks who is mainly intent on making fun, and who only makes mischief incidentally. Even the Robbers in the Cave are jovial fellows, who threaten wickedness, but do none of a serious kind, and they too enjoy their joke. This enjoyment of human weakness and folly was no characteristic of Smollett's. A French critic would probably account for the difference between master and pupil by the Protestant training, which, as our neighbours know, makes everybody so desperately serious. Whether the kirk had a direct influence on "Roderick Random" or no, is a large question, but Smollett was assuredly a very different man from Le Sage. He hated what the Frenchman laughed at, and would not pass over crimes and vices to enjoy folly. He found that the conduct of Gil Blas "not only deviates from probability, but prevents that generous indignation which ought to animate the reader against the sordid and vicious disposition of the world." This rider to his estimate of Le Sage's masterpiece points out with absolute accuracy exactly

why and where he differed from his master. A generous
indignation at the vicious disposition of the world was
not the gain which rewarded the student who discovered
the soul of the Licentiate Pedro Garcia. It was rather
an indisposition to be indignant at anything human, and
a willingness to look for the good there may be mixed
with the knavery and foibles of erring mankind. To
ask Smollett to take this kindly view would have been
as useless as to make the same demand on Swift.
Neither of them could ever cease to vex his soul
because of the unrighteous. Smollett avowedly meant
to be didactic, and that not by persuasion only.
He preferred to use the greater whip. "The impulses
of fear," as he puts it in the dedication to Doctor ——,
in "Count Fathom," "which is the most violent and
interesting of all the passions, remain longer than any
other upon the memory; and for one that is allured to
virtue by the contemplation of that peace and happiness
which it bestows, a hundred are deterred from the practice
of vice by that infamy and punishment to which it is
liable from the laws and regulations of mankind. Let
me not therefore be condemned for having chosen my
principal character from the purlieus of treachery and
fraud, when I declare my purpose to be to set him up
as a beacon for the benefit of the unexperienced and
unwary, who, from the perusal of these memoirs, may
learn to avoid the manifold snares with which we are
continually surrounded in the paths of life. While those
who hesitate on the brink of iniquity may be terrified
from plunging into that irremediable gulf by surveying
the deplorable fate of FERDINAND COUNT FATHOM."

Here is an avowal of an intention to purge by terror, if
not by pity, writ sufficiently large, and it is repeated in
the succeeding two paragraphs of the dedication.

In setting this didactic aim before himself, Smollett
departed from the practice of Le Sage, and reverted,
perhaps unconsciously, but undeniably, to the example
of the Spaniards. The mention of Spanish authors in
the preface to "Roderick Random" shows that·he at least
knew of the works of the writers of *novelas de picaros*.
Whether he had come across them in Spanish does not
appear. Probably not, for the fact that he translated
"Don Quixote" later on is no proof that he was master
of the language at the earlier date. But it was easy
for the English reader to be familiar with the *novelas
de picaros* without the smallest tincture of Castilian.
Mabbe had translated "Guzman de Alfaruche," in
Jacobean times, in a folio which will well repay reading,
text and marginal notes alike, and the Spanish rogue
had had a little English progeny of his own. Don
Diego Puede-ser [Puede-ser means "may be," and was
taken punningly as a *nom de guerre* by Mabbe] had had
followers. Roger L'Estrange translated "The Dreams"
of Quevedo, and the industrious but obscure Captain
Stevens, perhaps an old soldier of Peterborough's, had
followed after him again with other translations from the
Spanish. A modern critic of the more sagacious sort,
with a good nose for a plagiarism, might even find proof
of direct robbery, by Smollett, in the dedication of the
adventures of " Count Fathom." " I declare my purpose
is to set him up as a beacon," are words which can be
shown to be a robbery of Mateo Aleman, who called

his book, " The Beacon of Life," with quite as much
probability as has been shown for many alleged plagiarisms.
But without going into these delicacies we may acknow-
ledge readily that Smollett took the form of his three
stories from Le Sage, and that he had a certain kinship of
character with the Spaniards, who were Le Sage's models.
Into this old mould Smollett poured metal of his own.
His three stories have something which is distinctly his.
The portraiture of English seamanhood, is, for one thing,
very much his own, but it deserves to be taken by itself.
Before we can judge how far that portraiture was the
faithful transcript of an original, and how far it was an
artiotio picture in which the model is simply used as a
means of helping the painter in the expression of his own
artistic inclination, it is necessary to look at the books as
a whole, to see what was Smollett's method, and to settle
the preliminary question, how far his figures represent the
sitter, and how far they represent the painter.

Of the three, " Roderick Random " is by far the most
important; it is fresher and better reading than the other
two, and the method is the same. It is a material help
in the estimate of Smollett that so much of his first book
should be founded, not on life in general, but on his own
life. Here again Smollett has boldly supplied the evidence
for or against himself. " Every intelligent reader," so says
the already quoted preface, " will at first sight perceive I
have not deviated from nature in the facts, which are all
true in the main, although the circumstances are altered
and disguised, to avoid personal satire." This is a tacit
confession that, as Thackeray has said, Smollett began on
the opposite side from Fielding. He did not create a

5

character from a general observation of mankind. He took an individual man and put him in a novel, sufficiently altered and disguised to give the author a plausible excuse for saying that the original had no call to put the cap on. It is, with obvious differences, the manner of the authors of comedies of humours. They took a passion or a weakness, and put it in a human body. Smollett took an individual and made him into something which suited his immediate purpose.

The particular humours which a writer will select to make a personage out of will of course depend on his own character. Smollett, who wished to arouse a generous indignation in his readers' mind against the sordid and vicious disposition of the world, inevitably selected the hardest and darkest sides of human nature. An author cannot make you indignant with the sordid or vicious without showing it. He would look for it and even exaggerate it. What is called sometimes justly, but also a little indiscriminately, the brutality of Smollett, is, more often than not, due to the choice of his material for a purpose which to his own mind was distinctly humane. We could wish sometimes that he had laid to heart the banished Duke's warning to Jaques, and there may fairly be said to be something hard in the character of a man who dwells on odious things, even though it be for the purpose of showing them as hateful ; but there is obviously a wide difference between being merely somewhat indifferent to the pain which the display of brutality may excite in the reader's mind, and being indifferent to the brutality. If a man cannot endure the picture of the hardest sides of a hard time, he will certainly not enjoy

Smollett ; still these things were there, they were not all life, but they were an important part of it. The State trials give a picture of the condition of the prisons of those days which far surpasses anything that Smollett has written, and if he insisted too much on these and similar features of the life of his time, he was, at the worst, only to be blamed for want of perspective.

Remembering then what it was that Smollett sought for and what was his aim, we may know what to expect from "Roderick Random." His hero was to have been an orphan of " modest merit," struggling with the difficulties caused by " his own want of experience as well as from the selfishness, envy, malice, and base indifference of mankind." The theme lent itself to autobiography, and was doubtless chosen for that very reason. Smollett took the outline of his own life, and painted into it all the " selfishness, envy, and base indifference of mankind " he needed to produce the desired literary effect. Roderick is an orphan, like himself, but in an infinitely worse position. The grandfather, who " was remarkable for his abilities in the law, which he exercised with great success in the station of a judge, particularly against beggars, for whom he had a singular aversion ; " the cousin, " the young Actæon, who inherited his grandfather's antipathy to everything in distress," and who was wont to amuse himself by hunting Roderick with beagles ; the female cousins, who persecute the boy till he becomes too dangerous to touch, are the angry travesty of the Smollett family. The father's love match is the pathetic version of Archibald Smollett's rash marriage. The old judge's will answers to the disposition of his property

made by old Sir James.   In later times the author made
amends to his grandfather's house, but in 1748 he was in
another frame of mind; he knew well what he was doing,
and unquestionably he knew also that they would understand it at Bonhill.   As the story begins so it goes on.
The raw Scotchman's arrival in London, Mr. Cringer the
member of Parliament, and his friend Mr. Staytape the
tailor, the examining medical board and the admiralty yard,
were all parts of Smollett's experiences, told not as they
happened to him, but as they would best fit into the story.
The expedition to Carthagena, and the misfortunes of
his tragedy of James I. of Scotland, contributed their
share.   In this last there is probably even less deliberate
rearrangement of the material than in the description of
the household at Bonhill, and in spite of the disclaimer
in his preface, Smollett assuredly meant Brayer and
Sheerwit to recognize their portraits.   Indeed, the disclaimer must have served to draw attention to the personalities.   The young painter in Smollett's apologue,
which immediately follows his preface, was painfully
surprised when his friends thought themselves pointed
at in his conversation-piece, but then he did not call
his acquaintances together and say :—

"You observe, my friends, that my picture of Bruin as
an old toothless, drunken soldier, has a certain resemblance to our friend the captain; the owl perched upon
the handle of the coffee-pot with spectacles on his nose,
looking at that newspaper, may be taken by some for the
respectable Mr. B—— ; the ass, ornamented with a huge
tye wig, which, however, cannot conceal his long ears,

may be maliciously said to stand for poor C——; and ill-natured persons may think that D—— is aimed at in the picture of the monkey who appears with the implements of painting, but I assure you that I have not the least intention of ridiculing these good people."

This is precisely the line which Smollett took, and, like other gentlemen who have drawn a literary portrait, he was a great deal more anxious that the allusion should be clearly perceived than to escape the charge of making personal attacks.

The personalities of "Roderick Random" may have helped it to some *succès de scandale*, but this, as Smollett probably recognized later on, was no part of its good fortune. It was read then, and has been read ever since, by people who neither knew nor cared whether Lacy, or Rich, or Garrick, or Lyttelton were attacked in it or not. It has been loved and read and re-read because it is a vigorous and swinging tale of adventure. Roderick's transitions, though they are not like Gil Blas' " from distress to happiness, or at least ease," are equally sudden, and the reader is a great deal too much interested in the adventures to pity the hero, even if Roderick were an appropriate object for that kind of regard. Then the innumerable fantastic figures which fill the book live with a vivacious rather unnatural life of their own. Jackson, with his incurable Bohemianism; "my friend Banter," who welcomes his friend so gaily in the imaginary character of highwayman; Potion and Crab; Mr. Lavement, his wife and daughter; all the curious waggon-load of monstrosities who travel from Newcastle with the hero and his faithful friend Strap, remain in one's mind as something like the young painter's four figures in the conversation-piece.   They are hardly human beings, but they are wonderfully comic beasts in human shape.   Then the endless unresting comings and goings, the encounters of these strange masks one with another, keep up an unbroken stir which excites the reader as the actual sight of a pantomime might do—the pantomime one would wish to see performed by the wild, dancing figures of Callot, suddenly made flesh for our amusement.   It is the privilege of the master of narrative over the master of figure that he can make his ragged bullies with their truculent long swords sticking through their broken scabbards, and his skipping mountebanks with their inhumane long noses, his tatter-demalion beggars, and his wenches in mingled rags and finery, actually live and speak.   You must read the action into Callot or Hogarth for yourself, but in Smollett all that is supplied, and even the figure comes of itself.   There is never any doubt what any of the curious figures on his stage are meant to stand for ; their character is written very clearly on them, and they name one another as plainly as possible.

Unluckily, Smollett is not always quotable, and some of the more vivacious of his scenes must be left untouched, but here is one which, allowing for a certain eighteenth-century precision of language, may be taken without offence.   It is somewhat long, but that is easily pardonable :—

" The time between this event and dinner I passed in

observing a game of cards between two farmers, an exciseman, and a young fellow in a rusty gown and cassock, who, as I afterwards understood, was curate of a neighbouring parish. It was easy to perceive that the match was not equal, and that the two farmers, who were partners, had to do with a couple of sharpers, who stript them of all their cash in a very short time. But what surprised me very much was to hear this clergyman reply to one of the countrymen, who seemed to suspect of foul play, in these words : 'Damn me, friend, d'ye question my honour ? ' I did not at all wonder to find a cheat in canonicals, this being a character frequent in my own country ; but I was scandalized at the indecency of his behaviour, which appeared in the oaths that he swore, and the bawdy songs which he sung. At last, to make amends in some sort for the damage he had done to the unwary boors, he pulled out a fiddle from the lining of his gown, and promising to treat them at dinner, began to play most melodiously, singing in concert all the while. This good humour of the parson inspired the companions with so much glee that the farmers soon forgot their losses, and all present went to dancing in the yard. While we were agreeably amused in this manner, our musician, spying a horseman riding towards the inn, stopped all of a sudden, crying out, 'Gad so ! gentlemen, I beg your pardon ; there's our dog of a doctor coming into the inn.' He immediately concealed his instrument, and ran towards the gate, where he took hold of the vicar's bridle, and helped him off, inquiring very cordially into the state of his health. This rosy son of the Church, who might be about the age of fifty, having alighted and

trusted the curate with his horse, stalked with great
solemnity into the kitchen, where, sitting down by the
fire, he called for a bottle of ale and a pipe, scarce
deigning an answer to the submissive questions of those
who inquired about the welfare of his family. While he
indulged himself in this state amidst a profound silence,
the curate, approaching him with great reverence, asked
if he would not be pleased to honour us with his company at dinner? to which interrogation he answered in
the negative, saying, he had been to visit Squire Bumpkin,
who had drank himself into a high fever at the last
assizes; and that he had, on leaving his own house, told
Betty he should dine at home. Accordingly, when he
had made an end of his bottle and pipe, he rose and
moved, with prelatical dignity, to the door, where his
journeyman stood ready with his nag. He had no sooner
mounted than the facetious curate, coming into the
kitchen, held forth in this manner: 'There the old rascal
goes, and the devil go with him. You see how the
world wags, gentlemen. By Gad, this rogue of a vicar
does not deserve to live; and yet he has two livings
worth £400 per annum, while poor I am fain to do all
his drudgery, and ride twenty miles every Sunday to
preach, for what? why, truly, for £20 a year. I scorn
to boast of my own qualifications; but—comparisons are
odious—I should be glad to know how this swag-bellied
doctor deserves to be more at ease than me. He can
loll in his elbow-chair at home, indulge himself in the
best of victuals and wine, and enjoy the conversation of
Betty his housekeeper. You understand me, gentlemen.
Betty is the doctor's poor kinswoman, and a pretty girl

she is ; but no matter for that—ay, and a dutiful girl to
her parents, whom she visits regularly every year, though,
I must own, I could never learn in what county they
live. My service t' ye, gentlemen.' By this time, dinner
being ready, I waked my companion, and we ate
altogether with great cheerfulness. When our meal was
ended and every man's share of the reckoning adjusted,
the curate went out on pretence of some necessary
occasion, and, mounting his horse, left the two farmers to
satisfy the host in the best manner they could. We were
no sooner informed of this piece of finesse, than the
exciseman, who had been silent hitherto, began to open,
with a malicious grin, 'Ay, ay, this is an old trick of
Shuffle. I could not help smiling when he talked of
treating. You must know this is a very curious fellow ;
he picked up some scraps of learning while he served
young Lord Trifle at the University. But what he most
excels in is pimping. No man knows his talent better
than I ; for I was *valet-de-chambre* to Squire Tattle, an
intimate companion of Shuffle's lord. He got himself into
a scrape by pawning some of his lordship's clothes, on
which account he was turned away ; but as he was acquainted with some particular circumstances of my lord's
conduct, he did not care to exasperate him too much,
and so made interest for his receiving orders, and afterwards recommended him to the curacy which he now
enjoys. However, the fellow cannot be too much
admired for his dexterity in making a comfortable livelihood in spite of such a small allowance. You hear
he plays a good stick, and is really diverting company.
These qualifications make him agreeable wherever he

goes; and as for playing at cards, there is not a man within three counties a match for him. The truth is, he is a damnable cheat; and can shift a card with such address that it is impossible to discover him.' Here he was interrupted by one of the farmers, who asked why he had not justice enough to acquaint them with these particulars before they engaged in play? The exciseman replied without any hesitation that it was none of his business to intermeddle between man and man ; besides, he did not know they were ignorant of Shuffle's character, which was notorious to the whole country. This did not satisfy the other, who taxed him with abetting and assisting the curate's knavery, and insisted on having his share of the winnings returned; this demand the exciseman as positively refused, affirming that, whatsoever sleights Shuffle might practice on other occasions, he was very certain that he had played on the square with them, and would answer it before any bench in Christendom. So saying, he got up, and, having paid his reckoning, sneaked off. The landlord, thrusting his neck into the passage to see if he was gone, shook his head, saying, 'Ah ! Lord, help us ; if every sinner was to have his deserts—— Well, we victuallers must not disoblige the exciseman ; but I know what—if Parson Shuffle and he were weighed together, a straw thrown into either scale would make the balance kick the beam. But, masters, this is under the rose,' continued Boniface, with a whisper."

Here is a scene from a sordid and vicious world ; rogue or dupe, or rogue and dupe, is a description of every actor in it. Whether such a curate and such a vicar, such farmers and such a landlord, could have been found together in the England of the day, or at any time, is a question hardly worth discussing. They live in the England that Roderick Random saw. If Smollett had ever been called upon to defend his picture, he might have answered that if such things were not, they at least might be, and the best way of making them impossible was to excite the generous indignation of his readers against them. Whatever may be the truth of the picture, or the value of the writer's didactic purpose, the scene is given in admirable, vivacious prose. The characters pass the spot, to borrow a figure from Mr. Stevenson's "Treasure Island," with brisk activity and neatness of touch ; each of them labels the last speaker neatly, and is labelled in his turn, and the author's blows fall like the strokes of a strip-hammer. This passage is the more interesting in Smollett's work because it is one which had a distinct influence on a great master of the modern novel. It can hardly be doubted that Thackeray, who knew his " Roderick Random " well, and praised it often, had the curate of this scene in his memory when he drew Sampson—the very Bohemian parson in "The Virginians."

The hero who passes through this fantasmagoria is not an attractive personage. The "modest merit" of Smollett's orphan is much less obvious than the rascality of the world he has to struggle against. " Modest " and " merit " are two words which go very ill with such a personage as Roderick Random. Lady Mary Montague noted that her kinsman Fielding could never see that his heroes were pitiful fellows, and Smollett obviously died without realizing how nearly the hero, who was in some sort a portrait of himself, came to being a ruffian. The diffe-rence between Tom Jones and Roderick Random is partly a question of nationality. Jones is an English-man; he is a thick-skinned fellow enough, but he is good-natured; he will knock his enemy down with very little scruple, but once the offender is down Jones for-gives him. If he meets his worst foe in trouble, he will help him with ungrudging generosity. Random is a Scotchman, who, like Sir Walter Scott's drover, is not satisfied until he has drawn blood with the sword in his quarrels. If he helps an enemy, he throws his assistance at him, as Tom Jones would not have thrown a bone to a dog. To talk of him as indelicate, would be almost absurd — delicacy has nothing to do with Roderick Random. Neither need one look for consistency of character in this hero: any man who started with the nature and the training of Roderick Random would infallibly become a Barry Lyndon. But Roderick was not called upon to develop in any probable way. He is the central figure of a whirl of adventures, and it is enough that he fills his place with spirit. If he had been hanged, I, for my part, should have heard the tidings unmoved. When he marries Narcissa, and settles down to wealth, it is because the adventures are at an end, and one is sorry for it. For Roderick himself no human being can ever have been glad or sorry. The faithful Strap is more attractive, and it is just possible that four human beings may have competed for the honour of having sat for his portrait from some other motive than the desire to be put in a book. The valet is at least an honest figure of fun. His dog-like fidelity, his erratic courage, his patriotic confidence in Scotchmen, and in rogues who praise the Scotch, and his very scraps of Latin, give him more real vitality than his master. We feel that he at least deserved a better end, though it is the end of his fellow barber, and parcel Latinist, Partridge.

It is in keeping with Smollett's deliberate dwelling on the more brutal phases of life, that the would-be sentimental parts of his stories are so terribly forced, cold, and prosaically positive. We are told that the physician listened with complacency to the ravings of Renaldo, Count de Melville, over the loss of the peerless Monimia, ravished from him by the machinations of the wicked Fathom. At this distance of time we do not listen to him with complacency, nor indeed to any of the amorous parts of Smollett's work. When posterity reads that "the lovers were seated; he looked and lanquished; she flushed and faltered; all was doubt and delirium, fondness and flutter," posterity laughs. There is no love-scene in Smollett, though there are many which would be love-scenes if elaborate description and persistent filling up of adjectives could give them the spirit they lack. Nothing in all his work resembles even afar off that scene in Winchester Cathedral, when Esmond and his "beloved mistress" meet again, or the tragic appearance of Beatrix on the staircase at Walcot, "a woman whose eyes were fire, whose look was love, whose voice was the sweetest low song, whose shape was perfect symmetry, health, decision, activity, whose foot as it planted itself on the ground was firm and flexible, and

whose motion, whether rapid or slow, was always perfect
grace—agile as a nymph, lofty as a queen—now melting,
now imperious, now sarcastic—there was no single movement of hers but was beautiful." But such scenes are
rare. It would be easy to make a goodly list of masters
in romance, and even in poetry, who have never put
reality into their delineations of what Lord Bacon—
surely very strangely—called the weak passion of love.
Smollett is not alone in that deficiency. If he could
have left it alone his stories would have been free from
much pure boredom, or unconscious absurdity. He is
not worse than tiresome or ridiculous when he is driven
by the necessity of consulting the public taste, or misled
by ignorance of his own limitations, to deal with all that
side of life. Sir Walter Scott speaks of the lust of his
heroes, but the word is not so much too severe, as in-
appropriate. There is neither lust nor love in Smollett,
neither the noble nor the ignoble phases of the passion.
They are simply wanting, and instead of them there is,
as in so many of the Restoration comedies, a cold parade
of words—the laborious attempt of a clever writer to
supply mechanically the place of feeling. It looks very
gross now, but Smollett lived in an outspoken time,
which had no scruple about mentioning certains facts of
human nature. In these times other formulas have
taken the place of his. In 1748, and for long afterwards, readers did not feel shocked when the novelist
fairly put his characters to bed.

A writer who is painfully literal in his love scenes will
hardly be delicate in other respects. To this prosaic
accuracy of language ought to be attributed much of

what is called Smollett's brutality. He certainly describes and almost insists on the merely physical sufferings and weakness of mankind. Disease and deformity,
rags and vermin, are introduced by him with undesirable
frequency—undesired, that is, by the taste of our time.
Further, he is very apt to speak of mere brutal violence,
done either in jest or in anger, with little or no appearance of indignation on his own part. For one thing,
there are more blows given and received in Smollett;
there is more flogging than could be paralleled in the
work of any other writer who can fairly be called a man
of letters. His heroes inflict pain not only in revenge,
but even in mere jocularity, and there is no sign that
Smollett sees anything very blameworthy in their conduct. Peregrine Pickle tortures poor Pallet with absolute delight, and the author, though he does not represent
his hero as a model, never blames him for this part
of his behaviour. Several episodes both of "Roderick
Random" and "Peregrine Pickle" are full of mere human
cruelty, told with little or no comment and no effort to
draw a moral. A large school of modern novelists
have, superficially, shown the same indifference. Tour-
gueneff, to cite one name, never stops his narrative to
say this is cruel, or that is vicious. Flaubert records
the history of the misery and degradation of a whole
family with an appearance of absolute detachment. But
Smollett does not work in the same method as these
men. He is ready enough to intervene in his own
person and draw the moral for his reader. When he
does not do so, it may be at least plausibly contended
that he is not moved by the misery, or made indignant

by the barbarity which he describes. Even if he is not asked to show any personal feeling, he may still be blamed for dwelling unnecessarily on barbarous and horrible scenes. It may seem that he did not care enough to be unwilling to make use of any horror which he might find useful.

This callousness of Smollett has been often enough charged against him. M. Taine absolutely shrinks from him, and dismisses him in a note as a kind of unworthy appendix to Fielding; but this is a fit occasion for the use of the *distinguo*. It is easy to abuse the excuse which a writer's time makes for him, but it is an excuse and an explanation none the less. Smollett's contemporaries, even the most humane among them, did not find him blamably ferocious; they were not shocked by his unconcerned descriptions. Mrs. Delane and Lady Mary Montague, two very different women, read "Roderick Random" without being shocked. These two ladies were apparently of opinion that the things which he described were a part of life, and of the legitimate material of the novelist. It is of course one thing to say of Smollett that he was no more cruel than his time, and another to represent him as an exceptionally tender-hearted and kindly man. That he was this last nobody can well believe. No man deserving these epithets could have told the story of Miss Williams, or have given the picture of Captain Clewline and his wife in the debtors' prison, without a much more distinct expression of pity and horror than can be gathered from Smollett's narrative. Yet it would, I think, be manifestly absurd to accuse Smollett of indifference in these and many similar cases.

M. Taine, and he is not alone in his disability, cannot understand how any man could describe the misfortunes of Miss Williams in the unconcerned historic style of Smollett. It is disgusting to him, and not to him only, to see a woman sinking through inexpressible ignominy into Bridewell, to be lashed into attempting suicide, and flogged for the attempt. But, after all, it is necessary to distinguish between what was Smollett, and what was his time. It requires only a very superficial knowledge of the life of the eighteenth century, as shown in literature and in art, to be persuaded of the callous roughness of those times. Hogarth has done a history of Miss Williams of his own, which does not differ in any detail from Smollett's, except in the termination, which is more humane in the novel than in that well-known series of prints. Dr. Johnson was assuredly a humane man, and yet look at the comment which he made to Boswell on the story of Madame Lapouchin, the story that is to say which Lord Kames took from Chappe D'Auteroche. "The woman's life was spared, and no punishment was too great for the favourite of an Empress, who had conspired to dethrone her mistress." What the punishment was said to have been the reader may be left to learn from Lord Kames, or from Chappe D'Auteroche, or if he prefers it, from Marryat's " Pacha of Many Tales." If Smollett is to be blamed for barbarity, it must be because he thought less of it than his contemporaries, or dwelt on it more. That he is wholly invulnerable on this score I will not undertake to assert, but it must not be forgotten that his avowed object was to raise a generous indignation against the sordid and

6

vicious disposition of the world.   It was due to a certain
intellectual hardness which he shared with Swift, that he
did not see that the mere repetition of horrible things
was in itself an offence.   Fielding worked in the same
spirit, but it was with a kindliness of nature which made
him avoid mere repulsive detail.   Much of Smollett's
barbarity is pure and simple horse-play, which is certainly not a very dignified form of amusement, but need
not be taken too seriously.   Such a fool as Pallet would
be thought to deserve the treatment he received; nobody
was called upon to stop and ask himself whether the
painter *was* a possible human being, or only a mannikin
skipping about for his amusement.

Between the appearance of "Roderick Random" and
of "Peregrine Pickle," Smollett had paid a visit to France,
which left its traces on the second of these works.   He
travelled with his friend Moore, afterwards the author of
"Zeluco," and Smollett's own editor and biographer.
All the incidents of this tour, which have been preserved, have been used up in a praiseworthy business-
like way in "Peregrine Pickle."   The travellers fell in
with a party of exiled Scotch Jacobites, and also with an
English traveller who was to supply a good deal of "copy"
for the new novel.   In different ways both these meet-
ings touched Smollett's patriotism.   The melancholy
spectacle presented by Mr. Hunter of Burnside and his
fellow Scottish gentlemen brooding over their exile, and
wandering on the shore at Boulogne to get a look at the
cliffs of England, moved him very honestly; he felt and
wrote as he had done four years before, immediately
after the suppression of the rebellion—as a man who

was not a Jacobite, but who was Tory enough and Scotchman enough to feel for his unfortunate country-men. His power of drawing a vivid scene was never more kindly employed than in the description of the supper given by Peregrine to the four or five gentlemen who had been "exiled from their native homes in consequence of their adherence to an unfortunate and ruined cause," and who told him "that they were gone to the seaside, according to their daily practice, in order to indulge their longing eyes with a prospect of the white cliffs of Albion, which they must never more approach." The pathos of exile, the idle weary waiting, hopeless regrets, and the forced gaiety of men who have been driven from their country, are touched with all Smollett's dexterity, and more than his usual delicacy. It is noteworthy as a proof of how little the rancour of Englishmen endures, that this pathetic reference to the partisans of a lost cause was printed in London, without exciting anger or even comment, within five years of the suppression of the rebellion. Smollett might have remembered how boldly he had been allowed to speak for his countrymen while the memory of the black Wednesday, when the Highlanders were at Derby, was still fresh, before he wrote in his history that the English are "naturally fierce, impatient, and clamorous."

His English acquaintances in Paris left a much less genial trace on "Peregrine Pickle." Mark Akenside and his unnamed friend the painter were the originals of the physician and Pallet. What the author of the "Pleasures of Imagination" had done to offend Smollett is not very clear. If it is true that he made "disparaging remarks on Scotland," that would be enough to account for the unmeasured attack made on him. Perhaps, however, Akenside's real offence was, that he was not a little of a prig, and very much of a bore. He quoted Greek, he was a great republican, he laid down the law, and annoyed Smollett by continual talk about the ancients; at least this is what he did, if the physician is even a gross caricature of the real Mark Akenside. On the whole, one inclines to the belief that the physician was not more than a distorted portrait of a pragmatical gentleman who had the ill-luck to come in Smollett's way. There is a great deal of internal probability about the picture. What can be truer to a well-known type of character—never so familiar as in these days of ours—than the physician's appearance as a friend of humanity? Two French officers bully an innkeeper at Arras, whereupon this republican, after the manner of the ancients, comments as follows : " He said that the greatest man in Athens would have been condemned to perpetual exile, and seen his estate confiscated for public use had he dared, in such a licentious manner, to violate the rights of a fellow citizen ; and as to the little affronts to which a man may be subject from the petulance of the multitude, he [the humane physician to wit] looked upon them as glorious indications of liberty, which ought not to be repressed, and would at any time rejoice to find himself overthrown in a kennel by the insolence of a son of freedom, even though the fall should cost him a limb ; adding, by way of illustration, that the greatest pleasure he ever enjoyed was in seeing a dustman wilfully overturn a gentleman's coach, in which two ladies were bruised even

to the danger of their lives." This is caricature, but of a
perfectly legitimate kind. There is a type of philanthro-
pist who feels in that way, who experiences a virtuous
pleasure when some one is bruised, even to the danger
of his life, because another has been insolently treated
by quite different persons in a distant place. It is
erring in his own way, but only human to answer with
Pallet : " If that be the case, I wish you may see every
bone in your body broke by the first carman you meet
in the streets of London." The painter is more of a
fantoche than the physician, but he is distinctly a caricature of an ancestor of Thackeray's immortal Gandish.
His Cleopatra may hang in the same gallery as the
" Boadishia."

It is part of the history of " Peregrine Pickle " that the
first edition belongs to the class of books which are
chiefly known to the curious. Here no more need be
said about it than that Smollett apologized for it, and
removed much which even the by no means fastidious
taste of his time found offensive. For the rest, the " Peregrine Pickle " of literature is the edition which Smollett
revised, and finally gave to the world.

Smollett used up more than his experiences in " Peregrine Pickle." He not only shot into it all the bores
and fools who came in his way, which was legitimate,
but he gave one place, and, according to tradition and
probability, sold another, to persons who had nothing
whatever to do with the story. He tried, as it were, to
make journalism out of a novel. The long account of
the virtuous Mr. M—— was perhaps put in out of
friendship and admiration. The "melting Scot" had

been praised by Smollett in "Reproof," and perhaps as
a figure in the strange population of the Fleet he had
some right to stand among the other portraits of the
book. His story needs a great deal of annotating and
explaining. As it stands, it is much more a specimen of
eighteenth-century sensibility than a biography of Daniel
Mackercher, Esq. For the rest, what had that gentleman and the claimant to the Anglesea title to do with
"Peregrine Pickle"? From the literary point of view
nothing whatever, but Smollett cannot have troubled
himself at all about artistic consistency in this second
book of his. His wish to make it a success was manifestly strong, and the loose construction of a tale of
adventures allowed him to put in whatever might be
trusted to interest his public. As for the Lady of
Quality who divides the title-page with Peregrine Pickle,
her presence is susceptible of a very simple explanation.
There is no reason to doubt the story that Lady Vane
paid for her place, if only because no other excuse can
be given for her presence. The memoirs of a Lady of
Quality were openly advertised as a scandalous attraction
to the book. To most readers who were likely to be
drawn by such things, they must have been a sore
disappointment. Her ladyship is amusing as much for
what she does not say as for what she actually tells; but
her narrative is marked by a reticence of language which
might have been judiciously imitated by Smollett himself. Lady Mary Montague supposed that Smollett must,
in his character of "subaltern admirer" of Lady Vane,
have added some "strokes of humour." Lady Mary
was a judge of men, and women, and books. She

knew Lady Vane, and would be able to guess pretty accurately what she could and could not have written. It is for the rest probable enough that when Smollett undertook to bring out her memoirs, he also engaged to render them those services which Thackeray's Mr. FitzBoodle expected from one of Fraser's young men. But whatever work he may have rendered them as editor, the memoirs are distinctly Lady Vane's. Hardly any man could have written them, and assuredly Smollett could not. It is perhaps some excuse for their appearance in the book, that in Lady Mary's opinion " Her history, rightly considered, would be more instructive to young women than any sermon I know." They must have been very firmly convinced, in 1752, of the natural tendency of young women to wander from the straight path, if they saw any good in instructing them in the fortunes of Lady Vane as a warning. Lady Mary's comment is one proof among thousands of the belief of her time that all facts of life are proper to be talked of.

When its episodes are put aside, " Peregrine Pickle " is a tale of adventure on the lines of "Roderick Random," and written on the same method. It is more like "The Roman Comique," and less like "Gil Blas." There is more deliberate buffoonery, and rather less ferocity. Smollett was not going through something so nearly resembling his own life; he was less personally interested in the hero, and less wrath with his foes. As for the hero himself, his divine Emilia, his friend Crabtree, and the rest, they sadly need the help of Lamb's famous apology for the heroes and heroines of the Restoration comedy.

If they are to be judged as real people in a real world, then there is indeed not much to be said for them. Pickle is a ruffian, and Emilia is worthy of him, in spite of all her airs of virtue. That Smollett meant to be moral with his hero is clear, otherwise he would not have rebuked him at the hands of Gauntlet, or caused him to play such a poor figure in the scene Sir Walter could not away with. He is at pains to stop and say this was wrong in my hero; for that other offence of his he shall be duly punished and reformed by stripes; but when the castigation is over, and Peregrine is suddenly presented as a reformed character, he is, in fact, much the same Pickle that he was. In truth, change or persistency matter but little with them all, if, like Lady Vane's history, they are rightly considered. Look upon them as in a Utopia, if not of gallantry, though that is not wanting, yet of picaresque adventure, and they play their part right briskly. To ask them to be as the characters of Fielding is unreasonable; one might as well complain that Franca Trippa and Fritellino (to go back to Callot) are not in the least like the courtiers of Lewis XIII., and that the Balli de Sfessania gives no true picture of the Court of Florence. It is their function to supply a sanctuary and Alsatia wherein one may escape from the pressure of reality. To be sure, you may not like Alsatia. There are people who do not enjoy " The Roman Comique." To them "Roderick Random," and still more " Peregrine Pickle," can hardly be attractive. There is too much rude buffoonery and mere horse-play; but if a man does not object to this primitive form of humour, if he is not shocked or bored by the sight of

noisy human animals engaged in high jinks, then he can
enjoy them. For movement and what may be accurately
called "go," nothing can well be better than the hardly-
quotable story of the nymph of the road, whom Peregrine
Pickle proposed to turn into a young lady of fashion.
Her journey to the garrison with Pipes, the astounding
toilet which was prepared for her in the hall, and duly performed by the ex-boatswain's mate with tubs of warm water
and swabs of various texture, applied after the manner of
"the ceremony of scrubbing, as it is practised on board
of the king's ships of war," under the superintending eye
of Hatchway, and her subsequent startling appearance in
polite society, are all scenes from a literary Alsatia.
Nothing of the kind ever happened in this prosaic world,
but in the Utopia of adventures why should it not
happen? One feels that Smollett must have enjoyed
this episode most intensely himself; the style swings
along with such a fine, free movement, and the incidents
come tripping one after the other just as they bubbled
up in the author's brain. The man who cannot laugh at
it must be debarred from his amusement by something
other than the delicacy of his taste. Pickle's family
surroundings are more pleasant than Roderick's. Mrs.
Pickle is a fiend, but an incredible fiend, and can be
left on one side. Gamaliel Pickle the father, and
Mistress Grizzle Pickle, the first sketch of Tabitha
Bramble, are pure and wholesome fun; the other minor
characters are inferior to Roderick Random's gallery,
always excepting the famous garrison. As a picaresque
novel it is a little too much spun out, too much broken
by episodes, to be as good as its predecessor.

"Ferdinand, Count Fathom," which appeared in 1753, holds a very subordinate place in Smollett's works. Few readers will differ from Lady Mary's opinion that it showed a certain flagging in his "talent for invention." The beginning is indeed excellent. Defoe himself might have signed the portrait of Fathom's mother, the drunken, shameless, old camp follower. Her misdeeds and her death in the pursuit of her avocations—for she is shot while trying to murder a wounded officer on the field of battle—make a really memorable picture of the savage old military life of the seventeenth and eighteenth centuries. She herself lives in one's memory as a hideous, bloodthirsty, greedy old hag, with a quite horrible inability to realise her own wickedness; but she stands alone in the book. There is incident enough in " Count Fathom," but the story is forced. Smollett had obviously exhausted his experience and his vein. He worked on the same model with an effort which is painfully felt. The story gives a mere repetition of old scenes of roguery, written with scarcely a trace of Smollett's verve, and with no touch of his own colouring. It would be no great fault if Count Fathom, Count Melville, and the peerless Monimia were only unnatural, but they are colourless. They belong to the *genre ennuyeux* irredeemably. The incidents of seduction or robbery were the stock-in-trade of all writers of rogues' tales, and there is not a little which is mere echo from Smollett's earlier books. Doctor Chambers is greatly shocked by the Count, and could wish that Smollett had never written his history. It pains him to see such a bad man. The Doctor surely

shows his morality a little out of place. The Count is a
scoundrel, or, at least, tries to be one; but he is so weak,
so easily baffled, so utterly unable to succeed except
where he is helped by the incredible folly of the virtuous
characters; so much more in fact of a dupe than a villain,
that whatever feeling he does arouse is one of a rather
mild contempt. We hear much of his cleverness, but
never see it. Smollett's literary fault in connection
with him was not that he drew a greater sinner than any
man should put into a book, but that, having introduced
his hero as a villain of extraordinary ability, he entirely
fails to convince the reader that Count Fathom was
other than a very poor rogue indeed. The scene in the
Robbers' Hut in the forest is sometimes spoken of as
being original, and the model of many others of the
same kind, but the praise can hardly have been given
with the due recollection of much that is to be found in
the "Spanish and French Authors" whom Smollett took
as his masters. The didactic intention of the author is
continually obtruded, and the reader is asked incessantly
to observe what a villain Fathom is, and how wrong it is
to rob, lie, and be monstrously ungrateful. He that is
the reader is prepared to agree, but it is with a feeling
that he knew all this before, and does not think Ferdinand
Count Fathom quite interesting enough to repay him for
being told the commonplaces of morality over again.
Smollett's fierce indignation at sordid and vicious things
gives his narrative a certain gloomy vehemence; but the
incidents are so remote from anybody's possible experience that his denunciations are wasted in the air.

CHAPTER V.

THE convenient looseness of construction of these "Adventures" makes it permissible to pick Smollett's seamen and pictures of sea-life out of his work and take them by themselves. Indeed they insist on being taken apart, for they stand with a very bold relief in front of their background. What is best remembered in "Roderick Random" is the figure of Lieutenant Thomas Bowling and the expedition to Carthagena. Nothing in "Peregrine Pickle" can fairly compare with the garrison and its strange inhabitants. That favourite specimen of Smollett's humour, the supper after the manner of the ancients, is a grotesque caricature of pedantry, priggery, and fatuous imbecility, in the big style; but all its merits are to be found in the picture of Hawser Trunnion, Esq., and his following, and this has a breezy freedom which is wanting in the travesty of Akenside's real or imaginary follies. Smollett would unquestionably have left his record on the literature of his time if he had never gone to sea, but it would have been a different one; and if "English seamanhood" owes something to him to this day, for the portrait he drew of it, he was greatly its debtor for the unique opportunity it gave him of doing what no man had done before, and only one man has done since.

Great part as the sea has had in English life, and much as the sailor has been loved, they play but a small part in literature. The seaman was a recognized type when Chaucer wrote. His shipman is marked and moulded by his life as much as the " Frankelein " or the "Doctour of Phisike." He is a seaman of the fourteenth century, that is, a coaster. It was the "hote sommer" which had "made his hewe al broun," and not the gales of the ocean or the sun of the tropics. But though he had only hugged the coast from " Gotland to the Cape de Finis-terre," during the summer months, he was as much a man of the sea as Lieutenant Thomas Bowling. He had the marks of the sailor. He rode but ill, sticking on " as he coulde ; " he liked his " draught of win," and was not too scrupulous how he got it ; and, for he was a sea-man of the fourteenth century, he was a little of a pirate and gave no quarter. But after the shipman of the " Pilgrims," the sailor almost went out of literature until he came back with " Roderick Random." The boatswain of the " Tempest " and his men are from the sea un-doubtedly, but they only appear to disappear. It would be easy enough no doubt to find a long list of characters in plays or tales who are labelled "a ship captain," or "a pirate " ; but it would be proportionately difficult to single out one of whom it can be said that he has been formed by his life into a type differing from any known kind of landsman. The sea captain of the " Twelfth Night " is much such a gentleman as any of the others round the Duke. Fulke Greville has given an admirable

little sketch of a seaman, unwittingly, but not the less
vividly, in his account of Sir Philip Sidney's unsuccessful
attempt to join Drake in the great expedition against the
West Indies.   The Admiral's distrust of a fine gentleman, his determination to be " captain of his own ship,"
the touching air of frankness which covered his wily
manœuvres to get rid of Sir Philip, and his fine tough
regard for the interests of Frank Drake, are all as life-
like as they can be.   Touches like this are to be found
scattered in Elizabethan and later voyages, but they are
the material for a literary picture, and not a picture in
themselves.   Congreve indeed has drawn a sailor.   Ben
Legend, who, by the by, is both a tarpaulin and a
gentleman by birth, is manifestly no landsman.   He
has all the proper marks of the sailor.   His language is
full of maritime expressions of a kind.   The sea, he is
careful to tell everybody, is with him the rule, and the
shore the exception.   Ben thinks so little of longshore
affairs that he has even forgotten that brother Dick is
dead, and is entirely unmoved on being reminded of that
fact.   " Mess, that's true—marry, I had forgot.   Dick's
dead, as you say—Well and how ? " he says, and then
goes on to other matters.   He roves from port to port,
with a wife in each presumably.   " I love to roam about
from port to port, from land to land ; I could never
abide to lie port-bound as we call it," is his reason for
not marrying.   There is a smack of the forecastle in his
rebuke to Miss Prue.   Here at least there is a recog-
nition of a type, and an attempt to draw it.   Congreve
was not content to call his man a sea captain, or lieutenant, without giving him the character too, but after all

his Ben is a landsman's sailor, drawn by a man who was not familiar enough with more than the outside of the life to give vitality to the picture. A far less famous man than Congreve has indeed left a work which is an exception to the rule. C. Shadwell's "Fair Quaker of Deal; or, the Humours of the Fleet," is not only meant to be, but is, a living picture of seafaring men. Flip and Mizen are distinctly the forerunners of Oakum and Whiffle. Lieutenant Cribage and Lieutenant Easy are decidedly naval officers, to say nothing of being very amusing fellows. The play is full of curious touches of the old sea life; but still "The Fair Quaker" does not appreciably diminish Smollett's claim to originality. It stood much alone, and cannot be said to be famous, or indeed nearly so well known as it deserves to be. Wytcherley, who had been to sea, and under fire too, called his Manly and his Freeman, captain and lieutenant, but he did not even pretend to make them sailors. Defoe sends his heroes into salt water by preference, but no amount of voyaging can make seafaring men out of them. Captain Singleton is true to Defoe's general type of adventurer, a very good thing of its kind, but not a thing of the sea.

It looks somewhat wasteful in dramatists and story-tellers to neglect the wealth of good picturesque material which lay alongside of them, but, in truth, the mine was a very difficult one to work. The sailors and the sea life were so much apart from the experience of landsmen that they could not be really known to men of letters. To this day the separation is sufficiently marked. How few sailors are to be found in novels as compared to the

great host of army officers, and how colourless they are
when they do appear! Defoe could compile tales of
adventure from the numerous records of travel published
at the end of the seventeenth and beginning of the
eighteenth centuries ; but not having lived among them,
he could not give his sailors the individuality, and truth
he has given to Moll Flanders, and to the youth of
Colonel Jack. Before the sailor could be properly
drawn, it was necessary that a writer should come who
combined the faculty of telling a story of enduring
literary value, with personal knowledge of the sea.
There have—with all due respect to everybody be it
said—been but two novelists of whom as much can be
asserted. The one was the naval officer who drew Mr.
Chucks, Captain M——, and Mr. Midshipman Easy.
The other was the surgeon's mate who drew Lieutenant
Thomas Bowling, Jack Rattlin, Commodore Hawser
Trunnion, and his friend Jack Hatchway.

The sea life of " Roderick Random " makes so strange a
succession of scenes, that Smollett would appear to have
written them with an even greater tendency to exaggeration than any of the other parts of the adventures.
Probably, however, there is no part which is so nearly
literally true. There is some heightening of the colour
unquestionably. No captain can ever have cleared his
sick bay quite so brutally as Captain Oakham. No surgeon
was ever quite such a fool, coward, and ignorant lick-spittle
as Mackshane. No naval dandy can ever have been
quite so absurdly effeminate as Captain Whiffle. Even
if all the incidents which Smollett has introduced were
actually founded on fact, it is not likely that they can all

have happened in one ship within one short year. But if Smollett had chosen he could have made a key to "Roderick Random" every whit as convincing as the key to "Uncle Tom's Cabin." Mrs. Beecher Stowe's *pièces justificatives* have never been shaken. The utmost that can be said against them is, that they were raked together from all parts of the South, and from the records of many years, and that they give a false picture as a whole. Doubtless the same accusation could have been made against Smollett if he had cared to publish the evidence for "Roderick Random." But he could afford as well as Mrs. Beecher Stowe to support the criticism with equanimity. They both of them could allege that it was not their duty to report what had happened, but to draw a picture of what conceivably might happen. Nobody, who knows what little there is to be known about the internal life of the navy in the last century, can seriously doubt that a ship might well have been, to use the violent sea phrase, such a hell afloat as the *Thunder*.

Whether the deeds done in her were heightened by Smollett or no, there can be no question about the vividness of the picture of H.M.S. *Thunder*, 80. They answer very fairly to Dr. Johnson's famous description of a ship—a prison, in which you ran the additional risk of being drowned. Her officers had to pig in cabins formed by canvas partitions, barely large enough to give them room to turn in. They slept in hammocks, and their feeding is dreadful to hear of. The medical staff of H.M.'s ships and vessels of war would make "reflections suitable to the event" if their mess were such as Morgan

Thompson and Roderick Random had to be content with.

"We heard the boatswain pipe to dinner, and immediately the boy belonging to our mess ran to the locker, from whence he carried off a large wooden platter, and in a few minutes returned with it full of boiled peas, crying 'Scaldings' all the way as he came. The cloth, consisting of a piece of old sail, was instantly laid, covered with three plates, which, by the colour, I could with difficulty discern to be metal, and as many spoons of the same composition, two of which were curtailed in the handles, and the other abridged in the lip. Mr. Morgan himself enriched the mess with a lump of salt butter, scooped from an old gallipot, and a handful of onions, shorn, with some pounded pepper. I was not very much tempted with the appearance of this dish, of which, nevertheless, my messmates ate heartily, advising me to follow their example, as it was banyan-day, and we could have no meat till next noon."

Banyan days were Mondays, Wednesdays, and Fridays, on which no meat rations were served out. Salt junk was attainable, and out of it Morgan made the horrible compound called salmagundy, consisting of a slice of salt beef, taken straight from the brine, and mixed "with an equal quantity of onions, which seasoning, with a moderate proportion of pepper and salt, he brought it into a consistence with oil and vinegar." No wonder Random felt burnt up after a mouthful of this dreadful composition, and "endeavoured, with a deluge of small beer,

to allay the heat it occasioned." Small beer was still
served out to the fleet. Rum came in later, though it
was already drunk by the ward-room officers as a luxury,
and in the form of bumbo, which "is a liquor composed
of rum, sugar, water, and nutmeg." After the manner
of old drinks and old dishes, bumbo contained at least
two superfluous ingredients (not the rum, of course, nor
even the water) ; but it was a more human composition
than hipsy, a liquor much affected by Captain George
Shelvocke. This officer, who sailed to the South Seas
some twenty years before Vernon's expedition, and who,
among other feats, told the story of the albatross which
was the germ of the "Ancient Mariner," was wont, if his
enemy, William Betagh, captain of Marines, is to be
believed, to solace himself with a mixture of wine, water,
and brandy, praised, "by the admirers of it," as "meat,
drink, and cloth." Shelvocke thought this mixture good
for his gout, and loved it so well that he confiscated the
silver goblets supplied to the officers for their common
drinking by the owners of his privateer, the *Speedwell*,
and called up "the armourer to melt and hammer five of
them into circles to adorn the outside of a fine pail,
made by the cooper, for the more glorious drinking" of
his favourite vanity. Even Betagh acknowledges, however,
that Shelvocke ladled his drink out fairly. Smollett does
not mention the captain of the *Speedwell*, but he must have
had him and other heroes of the same stamp in his mind.
The boy who summoned Random's mess to their platter of
peas with cries of "scaldings," also ran round the decks
every morning, "ringing a small handbell, and in rhymes
composed for the occasion, invited all those who had

sores to repair before the mast, where one of the doctor's mates attended, with applications to dress them." Patients were not likely to be wanting when old and infirm men were mercilessly swept on board ship by the pressgang, and the Admiralty cared not how it composed the crews, provided it could fill up the complement. Miserable wretches, such as were driven on to the *Thunder's* deck from the sick bay, to be tortured to death by Oakum and Mackshane, might have been found at that very time on board of Anson's ship, the *Centurion.* The history of his famous voyage is indeed, as Carlyle called it, " a real Poem of its kind, or Romance all Fact; one of the pleasantest little Books in the World's Library at this date," but it is also a damning accusation of the men who governed England at that time.   If there is anything in the history of the Spaniards in South America more atrocious than the cruelty of the Ministry which filled Anson's vessels with decrepit veterans, and sent them round Cape Horn in winter, I do not know it, and do not want to hear it.   Cieza de Leon, who briefly records how his party went into a certain valley in the Andes, and took such a detestation to the people that they hung them up to the trees by the hair, and then marched away among dismal groans, with the firm belief that the souls of their victims would go to everlasting torment, may seem to have witnessed the most gratuitous piece of human barbarity ever committed.   It was none the less tender mercy compared to the sending of men, who had fought under Marlborough, to go round Cape Horn in the winter of 1740.   Only three of them lived to enter the Pacific, and none returned to England.

The story is worth remembering as one reads of the doings of Captain Oakum.

Men who ate salmagundy and drank bumbo were likely to be heated enough, and in such surroundings as theirs, whatever brutality there was in their nature would flourish as in a congenial soil. The midshipman Crampley and Captain Oakum remain as pictures, heightened, coloured, and exaggerated, perhaps, but essentially true, of the ruffianism of the sea. For Oakum one feels a certain respect. Brute as he is, he is a seaman and a brave man. You may hate the tyrant, but you cannot despise Oakum as he leans wounded against the mizen mast of his ship during the fury of the bombardment, sternly frowning at his doctor's disobedience to orders, and refusing to have his wound dressed by any man except the proper officer. It was pedantic of him, but it was courageous. Smollett, it may be observed, does not profess any love of the joys of battle. In the account of the accidental fight with the French ships off the coast of San Domingo, it is the horror of the scene which he dwells on. Roderick is certainly in a dreadful position, chained, helpless, on the deck, and covered with the blood of the men who fall round him ; but if Smollett had cared to see anything in battle but its horror, he would not have put his hero into that position, or have made him go mad for a time with fear and disgust. The deck of the *Thunder* during the bombardment is to him only "a most infernal scene of slaughter, fire, smoke, and uproar." Roderick Random's experience is like a first sketch of the picture of the *Victory's* quarter-deck given by her chaplain, who rushed up from below, unable

to stand the cockpit any longer, and found a pall of smoke
and of dust shattered out of the Spaniard alongside
hanging so low that the figures of Nelson and Hardy
walking up and down could barely be seen through it.
Smollett could admire courage, and show it too, but his
battles are always described from the outside, as if by a
literary man who was out of place in them, and was
mainly impressed by the dreadful side of war, its noise,
pain, and bloodshed.   There is nothing in his pages
answering to the capture of the Russian frigate in "Mr.
Midshipman Easy," when the English chaplain forgot he
was no longer a naval officer, and led the English
boarders.   Marryat, who was in more respects than one
Smollett's successor, had this advantage over him, that
he was a trained fighting man, writing of fighting.

The figure of Lieutenant Thomas Bowling is good to
put alongside of Captain Oakum.   He stands there to
represent all the best of the sea life.   Smollett never,
not even in "Humphrey Clinker," succeeded more completely in drawing a character, in creating a human being,
than he did with Random's uncle.   Bowling is empha-
tically a seaman, one of those men, who, like Anson,
had been round the world, but had never been in it.
He is childishly ignorant of the shore and its ways.   His
language is full of salt spray, and he has something of
the prodigal generosity of the race of men who made
their money like horses, and spent it like asses.   But
underneath Bowling's quaint outside there is a distinct
human character.   According to his lights, he has a keen
regard for his interests, and a very decided liking for his
own way.   It was foolish in him to rely on getting the

favour of the Admiralty Board by the peculiar influence
he felt so much confidence in, "For the beadle of the
Admiralty is my good friend, and he and one of the
under clerks are sworn brothers, and that under clerk
has a good deal to say with one of the upper clerks, who
is very well known to the under secretary, who upon his
recommendation, I hope will recommend my affair to the
first secretary, and he again will speak to one of the
Lords on my behalf; so that you see I do not want friends
to assist me on occasion." Roderick was not so clever
as he thought when he smiled at the ladder by which
his uncle "proposed to climb to the attention of the
Board of Admiralty," Lieutenant Dowling could have
found very good reasons for relying on those useful
persons, beadles, and under or upper clerks. From
the moment that Lieutenant Bowling gets on to his
own element again, his absurdities, which are, after
all, only differences of manner, entirely vanish. The
natural sagacity and courage of the man come out at
once. When he finds a place as mate to a Guinea trader,
he proves himself at once not only a good commander
and a resolute fighting man, but a sharp man of business.
This is perfectly true to the sea manners of a time when
the skipper and the merchant's agent were commonly
one and the same person, and when a man was chosen
to command, quite as much because he would know
what to do with the cargo, as for his capacity to sail the
ship. Bowling is an honest man; he would be incapable
of imitating the alleged dishonesty of Captain Shelvocke
the drinker of hipsy. This wily mariner took a Spaniard,
called the *Concepcion*, "Don Stephen de Recova,

commander," and reported that she was "laden with flour, sugar, marmalade (by which he meant quince cheeses no doubt), peaches, grapes, limes, *etcetera*," but, according to his enemy, Betagh, "*that etcetera, was, A hundred and eight thousand six hundred and thirty-six pieces of eight*," of which the owners might have taken it upon their conscience that at no period, and by no possible process, could one kreutzer be recovered. Lieutenant Bowling looked after his owner's business more honourably than Shelvocke is said to have done, but he belonged to the race of fighting, money-getting seamen of which Woodes Rogers, Dampier, Clipperton, and others of the end of the seventeenth and beginning of the eighteenth century, were ornaments. "I must do my uncle the justice to say," says Roderick Random in his condescending impudent manner, "that in the whole of his disposition he behaved with the utmost intrepidity, conduct, and deliberation." This was on the voyage to Buenos Ayres, when a fight with a big stranger appeared imminent. Of course Captain Bowling behaved with the utmost intrepidity, conduct, and deliberation. He also made a speech, and a very good speech too :—

"My lads, : : . I have gone to sea thirty years, man and boy, and never saw English sailors afraid before. Mayhap you think I want to expose you for the lucre of gain. Whosoever thinks so, thinks a damned lie, for my whole cargo is ensured; so that in case I should be taken, my loss would not be great. The enemy is stronger than we to be sure. What then? have we not a chance for carrying away one of her masts and so get clear of her? If we find her too hard for us, 'tis but striking at last. If any man is hurt in the engagement, I promise on the word of an honest seaman to make him a recompense according to his loss. So now you that are lazy, lubberly, cowardly dogs, get away and skulk in the hold and bread-room; and you that are jolly-boys, stand by me, and let us give one broadside for the honour of Old England."

No wonder they were ready to fight after that, for it was both good sense and courage. In a rougher and more prosaic, but not less valiant way, it is as good as the real speech made by Captain Best, of the East India Company's Service, when he was threatened by an apparently overwhelming Portuguese force at Surat, in 1612. Best was a man of the early seventeenth century, probably something of the Puritan, and certainly more apt to quote the Bible than they were about 1740. He read Psalm xvi. to the crew of the *Hoseander*, beginning at the eighth verse. The rest of his address was more after the manner of Lieutenant Bowling's. After showing the obvious connection between these verses, and the necessity there was for smashing the Portuguese, "he further told them that if it should please God that any of our men in fight were dismembered or lamed, he faithfully promised upon his credit and reputation, in the hearing of the company, that he would be a means unto the Worshipful (Company) whom we serve, in their behalf for reasonable maintenance to keep them as long as it should please God they live." After spiritual exhortation and solid business-like encouragement, Captain

Best, having ended his speech, "took a cup of wine and drank to the master and all the company, and desired God to give us His Blessing, and so returned aboard his own ship to sermon." With the help of Sermons, dinner, cups of wine drunk to one another, and the good example of Captain Best, the *Hoseander* and her consort gave a very good account of the Portuguese.

Captain Bowling belonged to the same race as that Captain Walton, who commanded the *Canterbury*, in the Mediterranean, under Byng—the elder Byng, the one who beat the enemy and was not shot. This admirable officer wrote the famous despatch which has been often quoted, but is not so well known that it may not be fairly quoted again.

"Sir,—We have taken and destroyed all the Spanish ships and vessels which were upon the coast, the number as per margin.

"I am, etc.,
"G. Walton.
"*Canterbury*, off Syracusa,
"*August* 16, 1718."

In 1718, Thomas Bowling had just about done learning how to splice a rope and raise a perpendicular. If Roderick Random had swung at the yardarm of the *Thunder*, it would have been no great matter, but one is glad to know that his uncle ended with wealth and in command. The typical good seaman has his following and companion figures. Jack Rattlin, who is Bowling before the mast, and Brayl, Roderick's messmate on the

Lizard sloop, who "much resembled my uncle both in figure and disposition," and was "a diligent and excellent officer," are there to counter-balance Oakum's kindred spirits, Crampley and Mackshane.

The group of seamen in "Peregrine Pickle" are less of an actual picture of life. Smollett manifestly did not so much draw on his experience for Trunnion, Hatchway, and Pipes, as deliberately set to work to make comic figures out of the materials afforded him by the real or even the imaginary eccentricities of the seamen. Nor that even here there is not a very real basis of truth under the fantastic superstructure. Whoever has enjoyed the society of retired naval, and even military gentlemen, has surely heard something very like the furious comments of the commodore on the promotion of Admiral Bower. Lieutenant Hatchway, "with an elevation of voice, that seemed to prognosticate something extraordinary," read the dreadful announcement of the admiral's approaching elevation to the peerage. "Trunnion was thunderstruck at this piece of intelligence. The mug dropped from his hand and shivered into a thousand pieces, his eye glistened like that of a rattle-snake, and some minutes elapsed before he could pronounce, ' Avast, overhaul that article again.'" When the shameful report is confirmed, how nobly does Trunnion denounce woe to a whole nation which can promote Will Bower and lay Hawser Trunnion on the shelf : " If so be as this be the case, there is a rotten plank in our constitution, which ought to be hove down and repaired." Neither is the commodore's oblivion of the fact that he has told the story of his action with the *Flour de Louse*,

a French man-of-war—" every watch for these ten
months past," by any means unnatural or forced. Still
Hawser Trunnion, take him altogether, is larger than life.
His striking resemblance to the wooden lion that used to
stand at his gate, and the vehemence of his language, are
both a little too highly coloured for sober art. As for
the language, it is on a Gargantuan scale : Trunnion no
sooner heard Mr. Hatchway mention the cause of
Grizzle Pickle's disorder, "than his morosity recurring, he
burst out into a violent fit of cursing, and forthwith
betook himself again to his hammock, where he lay
uttering, in a low growling tone of voice, a repetition of
oaths and imprecations for the space of four-and-twenty
hours without ceasing." Trunnion is, in fact, a huge mass
of violence, simplicity, and ignorance, played upon by
that practical joker Hatchway, and dragged through all
kinds of violent misadventures to make fun for the
reader. The ride to church is a companion scene to the
supper after the manner of the ancients, an outbreak of
horseplay and loud animal laughter. As the story goes
on Smollett seems to have undergone some such change
of feeling in regard to Trunnion as Cervantes felt
towards Don Quixote, and Dickens to Mr. Pickwick.
He began by meaning to make him merely absurd, he
ended by liking him. In the earlier chapters Trunnion's
fury is represented as the violence of a braggart. He
has hardly done boasting of the wounds he has received
in the service, before the malicious Hatchway gives a
loose to his satirical talent once more, saying, " I have
heard as how you came by your lame foot, by having
your upper decks over-stowed with liquor, whereby you

became crank, and rolled d'ye see, in such a manner, that by a pitch of the ship, your starboard heel was jammed in one of the scuppers ; and as for the matter of your eye, that was knocked out by your own crew when the *Lightning* was paid off. There's poor Pipes who was beaten into all the colours of the rainbow for taking your part and giving you time to sheer off ; and I don't find as how you have rewarded him according as he deserves." The commodore could not deny the truth of these stories. His great action with the *Flour de Louse* remains somewhat obscure, but it is very certain that he did not take the Frenchman. Later on in the story there is no doubt about the commodore's courage, and he becomes humanized. There is a real tenderness in the picture of the old man's love for his scamp of a nephew. His mere violence and fury are greatly toned down, and at the end he really becomes very pathetic. His wish to be buried in "the red jacket which I wore when I boarded the *Renummy*," is in perfect keeping with the character of the rough old hero. One cannot laugh even at the epitaph written for him by Hatchway.

"Here lies,
Foundered in a fathom and half,
The shell
of
HAWSER TRUNNION, ESQ.,
Formerly commander of a squadron
In his Majesty's service,
Who broached to, at five P.M., Oct. x.
In the year of his age
Three score and nineteen.

He kept his guns always loaded,
And his tackle ready manned,
And never showed his poop to the enemy,
Except when he took her in tow:

But
His shot being expended,
His match burnt out,
And his upper works decayed,
He was sunk
By Death's superior weight of metal.
Nevertheless
He will be weighed again
At the Great Day,
His rigging refitted,
And his timbers repaired;
And, with one broadside,
Make his adversary
Strike in his turn.

The commodore, one is persuaded, deserved the praise on his tombstone. His friend Hatchway and his retainer Pipes shine by reflection from him. When Trunnion is gone, the lieutenant's function in life is nearly done; he remains there to keep the garrison for Pickle, but the place loses almost all its interest when its ditch and palisade and patereroes no longer protect the little fragment of the old navy formed of the commodore and the survivors of the crews with which he fought the *Triumph,* the *Flour de Louse,* and the *Renummy.*

CHAPTER VI.

THE publication of "Ferdinand, Count Fathom,"
marked the end of Smollett's first productive
period of novel writing, and the beginning of many years
of arduous work done for pay. He had not given up all
hope of finding a crutch in medicine. In 1750 he
obtained a degree of M.D. from the Marischal College
of Aberdeen. Dugald Dalgetty's Alma Mater could give
him a degree, but could not give him a practice; and
yet he tried so hard to establish a reputation as a medical
man by the publication of a scientific treatise on the
external use of water. The enterprize is enough in
itself to explain why Smollett never succeeded as a
doctor. The water he wrote about was the water of
Bath, and his object in the treatise was apparently to
prove that any other water would do every bit as well.
If, as may be supposed, he was trying to establish himself at Bath, this was hardly the way to go to work to
make himself popular. That he ever did try to obtain
a practice at Bath is hardly more than mere matter of
guess-work. He was certainly very fond of the town;
he introduces it into all three of his first novels, and
went back to it in his last. The medical life of the

place, and in particular its quackery, had an endless attraction for him, but his descriptions are enough to account for his failure as a doctor. A gentleman who has called the whole medical profession quacks and fools in print, and has supplied many thousands of possible patients with the material wherewith to make fun of their medical men, can hardly come forward and present himself as a possible family doctor with a very good grace. The faculty may forgive him, but the patients are tolerably sure to think that such a funny gentleman is not nearly serious enough for the place. Nothing shows Smollett's consciousness of the rectitude of his intentions better than the innocent belief that the author of " Roderick Random " and " Peregrine Pickle " could ever get established in practice.

With whatever degree of unwillingness, and whatever occasional efforts to go into another path, Smollett had now to settle down to incessant literary labour. Either in 1752, or not long after it, he took the house described in " Humphrey Clinker," which he seems to have continued to occupy to the end of his life in London. This was Monmouth House, in Lawrence Street, which must have had a national interest for him, for it had been occupied, if not owned, by that Anne Scott who married the wretched Monmouth, and who was the ancestress of the present House of Buccleuch. Of Smollett's personal habits very little is known, and the want of details must always deprive a biography of much of its best interest. The comparative obscurity of Smollett's life in a generation so abundantly well-known as his, is partly, no doubt, due to the fact that he did not belong to the society that gathered round Dr. Johnson. He never came sufficiently in Boswell's way to have the good fortune of sitting for his portrait to that master draughtsman. In 1763, when Boswell first met his illustrious friend in Davies' shop, Smollett was just about setting out on his travels through France and Italy, and from that time he was little in London. It would hardly have been possible for any man to have lived in the literary world of that day without coming across Johnson; and Smollett had some dealings with the great "Cham of Literature." It is one of the best-known facts of his life that he applied to Wilkes to secure the release of "the great lexicographer's" black servant, who had been pressed on board the *Star* frigate; but this is hardly proof that Smollett and Johnson were even acquainted. The Scotchman may have been asked to exert himself by some common friend who knew that he was on good terms with Wilkes. In any case, however, it is probable that Smollett would not have been much known. His work seems to have wrapped him up very closely. He is even said never to have left his house while he was engaged on his history, and his multifarious engagements as a translator or journalist must have kept him very closely to his desk. Dr. Johnson's social life was made easier for him by his pension. But the necessity of working for his bread and butter would not of itself have kept Smollett apart in the literary world. Hard as it was, other men did nearly as much, and yet contrived to see a great deal of one another. The truth would seem to be that Smollett was not an easy man to know, or to live with. Doctor John

Moore, his·friend and countryman, has praised him in general terms for being "of a disposition so humane and generous that he was ever ready to serve the unfortunate, and on some occasions to assist them beyond what his circumstances could justify." This is a praiseworthy disposition no doubt, but it is perfectly consistent with a character which would keep a man apart from the more independent of his contemporaries. It is possible to combine a generous readiness to help the unfortunate with a distinct preference for having the persons you have obliged about you, and Smollett does seem, on his own showing, to have enjoyed the dignity of possessing a little senate of his own. Certainly he has himself to blame if this is the general impression we get about him. A man's descriptions of himself are proverbially untrustworthy as evidence of what he was, but they are a tolerably safe guide to a knowledge of what he wanted to be. Now Smollett has twice introduced himself to the public with an astonishing frankness. First, in a general way, in the preface to "Ferdinand, Count Fathom," and then with more detail in "Humphrey Clinker." The dedication to Dr. ——, gives Smollett's view of Smollett with a charming air of sincerity. "Know, then," he says to himself, after some preliminary flourish, "I can despise your pride, while I honour your integrity; and applaud your taste, while I am shocked at your ostentation. I have known you trifling, superficial, and obstinate in dispute; meanly jealous and awkwardly reserved; rash and haughty in your resentments; and coarse and lowly in your connections. I have blushed at the weakness of your conversation, and trembled at the errors of your conduct. Yet, as I own, you possess certain good qualities, which overbalance these defects, and distinguish you on this occasion as a person for whom I have the most perfect attachment and esteem; you have no cause to complain of the indelicacy with which your faults are reprehended, and as they are chiefly the excesses of a sanguine disposition and looseness of thought, impatient of caution or control, you may, thus stimulated, watch over your intemperance and infirmity with redoubled vigilance and considera-tion, and for the future profit by the severity of my reproof."

This may be fairly taken to mean that when Smollett descended into himself, he analyzed his own character as that of a rather overbearing, masterful person, and, on the whole, he was not ill-pleased with his own appear-ance. From a hundred touches in his novels and in his travels, it is clear that he was not a man to doubt whether he did well to be angry. With such a disposition life would be easier to him if he was surrounded by depen-dents. He would even be inclined to overlook the worthlessness of men whom he chose to befriend, as long as they were in need of his help. It is cynical, no doubt, to enjoy the spectacle of human meanness, but cynicism has its attractions, and Smollett had early made up his mind that the greater part of human nature was composed of meanness, and had reconciled himself not so much to tolerate it as to rage at it, despise it, and live with it for want of better. The one set off he did require to meanness was, that it should be subordinate to himself. This, at least, is the account of himself which he set

Jerry Melford to draw up in later years, and it may be quoted here, though a little before its time :—

"He [Smollett] lives in the skirts of the town, and every Sunday his house is open to all unfortunate brothers of the quill, whom he treats with beef, pudding, and potatoes, port, punch, and Calvert's entire butt beer. He has fixed on the first day of the week for the exercise of his hospitality, because some of his guests could not enjoy it on any other, for reasons that I need not explain. I was civilly received, in a plain, yet decent, habitation, which opened backwards into a very pleasant garden, kept in excellent order ; and indeed, I saw none of the outward signs of authorship, either in the house or in the landlord, who is one of those few writers of the age that stand on their own foundation, without patronage and above dependence. If there was nothing characteristic about the entertainer, the company made ample amends for his want of singularity.

"At two in the afternoon, I found myself one of ten messmates seated at table ; and I question if the whole world could produce such another assemblage of originals. Among their peculiarities I do not mention those of dress, which may be purely accidental. What struck me were oddities originally produced by affectation, and afterwards confirmed by habit. One of them wore spectacles at dinner, and another his hat flapped ; though, as Ivy told me, the first was noted for having a seaman's eye when a bailiff was in the wind, and the other was never known to labour under any weakness or defect of vision, except about five years ago, when he was complimented with a couple of black eyes by a player with whom he had quarrelled in his drink. A third wore a laced stocking, and made use of crutches, because once in his life he had been laid up with a broken leg, though no man could leap over a stick with more agility. A fourth had contracted such an antipathy to the country, that he insisted on sitting with his back towards the window that looked into the garden; and when a dish of cauliflower was set on the table, he snuffed up volatile salts to keep him from fainting. Yet this delicate person was the son of a cottager, born under a hedge, and many years had run wild among geese on a common. A fifth affected distraction. When spoken to he always answered from the purpose : sometimes he suddenly started up and rapped out a dreadful oath; sometimes he burst out a laughing; then he folded his arms, and sighed; and then he hissed like fifty serpents.

"At first, I really thought he was mad, and, as he sat near me, began to be under some apprehensions for my own safety, when our landlord, peceiving me alarmed, assured me, aloud, that I had nothing to fear. 'The gentleman,' said he, 'is trying to act a part for which he is by no means qualified; if he had all the inclination in the world it is not in his power to be mad. His spirits are too flat to be kindled into frenzy.' ''Tis no bad p-p-puff, how-ow-ever,' observed a person in a tarnished laced coat, 'aff-ffected m-madness w-will p-pass for w-wit, w-with nine-nine-teen out of t-twenty.' 'And affected stuttering for humour,' replied our landlord, 'though, God knows, there is no affinity between them.'

It seems this wag, after having made some abortive attempts in plain speaking, had recourse to this defect, by means of which he frequently extorted the laugh of the company, with the least expense of genius; and that imperfection which he had first counterfeited was now become so habitual that he could not lay it aside.

"A certain winking genius, who wore yellow gloves at dinner, had, on his first introduction, taken such offence at S——, because he looked and talked, and ate and drank like any other man, that he spoke contemptuously of his understanding ever after, and never would repeat his visit until he had exhibited the following proof of his caprice. Wat Wyvil, the poet, having made some unsuccessful advances towards an intimacy with S——, at last gave him to understand, by a third person, that he had written a poem in his praise, and a satire against his person; that if he would admit him to his house, the first should be immediately sent to the press, but that if he persisted in declining his friendship he would publish the satire without delay. S—— replied, that he looked on Wyvil's panegyric as, in effect, a species of infamy, and would resent it accordingly with a good cudgel; but if he published the satire, he might deserve his compassion, and had nothing to fear from his revenge. Wyvil, having considered the alternative, resolved to mortify S—— by printing the panegyric, for which he received a sound drubbing; then he swore the peace against the aggressor, who, in order to avoid a prosecution at law, admitted him to his good graces. It was the singularity in S——'s conduct on this occasion that reconciled him to the yellow-gloved philosopher, who owned he had some genius, and from that period cultivated his acquaintance.

" Curious to know on what subjects the several talents of my fellow-guests were employed, I applied to my communicative friend, Dick Foy, who gave me to understand that most of them were, or had been, understrappers or journeymen to more creditable authors, for whom they translated, collated, and compiled, in the business of bookmaking; and that all of them had, at different times, laboured in the service of our landlord, though they had now set up for themselves in various departments of literature. Not only their talents, but also their nations and dialects were so various, that our conversation resembled the confusion of tongues at Babel."

The rest of this, "the most diverting of young Melford's letters to Sir Watkin Philips," as Lockhart has called it, describes the Sunday guests at Doctor S——'s house, and a very curious party they make. There is the philosopher, who had been expelled from the university for atheism, and had lately been interrupted in his ingenious and orthodox refutation of Lord Bolingbroke, by a prosecution for blasphemy at an alehouse on the Lord's Day; there was the Scotchman, who gave lectures on pronunciation of English; my lord Potato, the Irish politician; the Piedmontese critic of English poetry, and other "ragged tenants of Grub Street." At the head of the table, Doctor S—— sat, to keep order and exert "a sort of paternal authority over this irritable tribe." This scene very naturally recurred to Lockhart's mind when he repeated the accounts which John Ballantyne had given him of the dinners with which Constable "regaled, among others, his own circle of literary serfs," at his house at Polton. The race between Jim Cropdale and Mr. Birkin for a bowl of punch, to be drunk at Ashley's in the evening, has its equivalent in the race between "poor Allister Campbell and another drudge of the same class for a new pair of breeches." Lockhart gives the story of the practical jokes at Polton, on John Ballantyne's authority, and with the warning that they may be overcharged. Perhaps they were, and perhaps, also, Smollett overcoloured his picture also, but Ballantyne was telling tales of a man for whom he had no real liking, while Smollett describes himself. This makes a difference in the value of the two sketches as evidence. Whether the publisher ever made fun of the folly and poverty of his guests may be doubtful, but there is no doubt that the novelist chose to represent himself as making "copy" out of the misery and meanness of men whom he had invited to his house. The picture is not altogether a pleasant one. It is evidence of the existence of a certain insolence in Smollett's character in the middle years of his life, and it helps to explain why he seems to have seen so little of the great literary world of his time, and to have been apparently so little liked by it.

That Smollett's picture of himself is no imaginary one, may be considered as proved by the same Doctor Carlyle who has been already quoted. In 1758 the Doctor was in London, and had looked his friend up again :

" Robertson (the historian) had never seen Smollett, and was very desirous of his acquaintance. By this time the Doctor had retired to Chelsea, and came seldom to town. Home and I, however, found that he came once a week to Forrest's Coffee House, and sometimes dined there, so we managed an appointment with him on his day, when he agreed to dine with us. He was now become a great man, and being much of a humourist, was not to be put out of his way. Home and Robertson and Smith and I met him there when he had several of his minions about him, to whom he prescribed tasks of translation, compilation, or abridgment, which after he had seen he recommended to the booksellers. We dined together, and Smollett was very brilliant. Having to stay all night, that we might spend the evening together, he only begged leave to withdraw for an hour, that he might give audience to his myrmidons ; we insisted that if his business [permitted], it should be in the room where we sat. The Doctor agreed, and the authors were introduced to the number of five, I think, most of whom were soon dismissed. He kept two, however, to supper, whispering to us that he believed they would amuse us, which they certainly did, for they were curious characters.

"We passed a very pleasant and joyful evening. When we broke up, Robertson expressed great surprise at the polished and agreeable manners and the great urbanity of his conversation. He had imagined, that a man's manners must bear a likeness to his books, and as Smollett had described so well the characters of ruffians and profligates, that he must of course resemble them. This was not the first instance we had of the rawness in respect of the world that still blunted our sagacious friend's observations."

Here at least is confirmation of the supposition that Smollett lived much by himself, and had his dealings mainly with dependents.

The history of a man who shut himself up to labour, and saw little society except that of hangers-on and drudges, would be naturally the history of his works. To be sure this is abundant enough for the next ten years of Smollett's life. Between 1752, when he settled at Chelsea, and 1763, when he went abroad on his travels, Smollett was always engaged in carrying on several literary undertakings abreast of one another, and as the years went on the press of work became more severe. He was at once an author engaged in filling a long shelf, and an active journalist. A goodly list of quarrels may be added to his other labours; all three, the literature, the journalism, and the quarrels, were connected with one another, and they became crossed and mingled until it is by no means easy to give an unconfused account of them. Perhaps the most convenient starting-point for an account of these years will be found in one of the quarrels, which does not appear to have arisen out of his literary work. Smollett had been connected in some way, apparently a charitable one, with an unfortunate creature of the name of Peter Gordon. Gordon was not only unfortunate, but if Smollett's version of the story is to be believed, dishonest and ungrateful. The novelist had helped him with his purse. In order to get rid of the debt, the debtor took refuge in 1753 in the liberties of the King's

Bench Prison, and from that strength, as Cuddie Headrigg
would have called it, sent contumacious messages to his
benefactor. Smollett hereupon gave him a thrashing.
This course he was always very apt to take.   In his travels
through France and Italy he tells many stories of his own
ludicrous promptitude in threatening offenders with his
cane, generally with more or less unfortunate results to
himself.   On the present occasion the assault entailed on
him very unpleasant trouble indeed.   Gordon brought
an action against his assailant, and secured the services
of a Mr. Hume Campbell as counsel.   This barrister
seems to have been, although he was a man of good
family connections, an Old Bailey practitioner of the loud-
mouthed bullying kind.   He did his best to turn an
ordinary assault into something like an attempt to murder,
and he not only cross-examined Smollett's witnesses with
great severity, but said many violent things to the jury
about Smollett himself.   Mr. Campbell failed to persuade
the jury that there had been an attempt to murder, but
about the assault there could be no doubt, and Smollett
was compelled to make a composition by which he was
bound to pay Gordon's legal expenses, and which
burdened him with a heavy bill at a time when his
affairs were by no means flourishing; and he was furiously
aggravated by the language of Mr. Hume Campbell.
While he was smarting under the double provocation, he
wrote a very long and very angry letter to the barrister.
He asked Mr. Hume Campbell, at great length, how he
dared to use such unbecoming language, or to praise his
own ignoble client in such a scandalous manner.   He
asked him pointedly whether certain passages describing

the infamous conduct of lawyers in " Ferdinand, Count Fathom," did not come home to his conscience. In short, he gave Mr. Hume Campbell a severe wigging, and challenged him to fight. No duel, however, or any other consequence followed from this letter ; it is even doubtful whether it ever reached the person to whom it was addressed. It was printed in 1784, in *The European Magazine,* from a rough draft which seems to have been sent to Daniel Mackercher, the Mr. M—— of " Peregrine Pickle." If Mackercher deserves all the praise lavished on him by Smollett, as a zealous and judicious friend, he must have advised that the letter should be put into the waste-paper basket. To challenge an English barrister, who was of a sufficiently low type to abuse the privileges of the bar, for language used in court, might have brought on Smollett legal proceedings even more disagreeable than Mr. Peter Gordon's. From the fact that nothing more is heard of the quarrel, it is probable that Smollett took the course which wise men have been known to recommend to authors who think themselves aggrieved by criticism. He wrote an angry letter to relieve his feelings, and avoided further wrangling by not sending it.

While the Peter Gordon quarrel was in progress, Smollett was at work on the translation of " Don Quixote," which appeared in 1755. This was the first of the works published during what may be called his second period of activity—the period during which he almost wholly ceased to produce original, imaginative work, and devoted himself to literary labour of a business-like kind. It was followed in 1757 by a " Compendium of

Voyages," edited by him, and to which he contributed the already quoted account of Vernon's expedition to Carthagena ; in the same year he did at last make his way on to the stage, for the first and only time, with a comedy called " The Reprisal; or, The Tars of Old England," whereof more anon. In this same busy year appeared the four quarto volumes of his " History of England " from the invasion of Julius Cæsar to the Peace of Aix la Chapelle, to be followed in the next year by a revised edition, published in monthly numbers, at the price of one shilling each, and to be continued to the year 1762, ten years later. In 1758–60 he was at work rather as editor than contributor, on a " Modern Universal History." In the last of these three years he was employed again, mainly as editor and annotator, along with a certain Doctor Francklin and others, on a translation of the complete works of Voltaire. Another business compilation of the same kind as the " Universal History " was " The Present State of all Nations," which also comes into 1760. In the meantime he had been pretty steadily engaged on *The Critical Review* from 1756 and onwards. In 1760, either in addition or as a substitute to the *Critical*, he became connected with *The British Review* for which he wrote " Sir Launcelot Greaves," a story notable as one of the first, if not the very first ever published in parts in a periodical.

This very respectable spell of work was twice interrupted. In 1755, very shortly after the appearance of the " Don Quixote," Smollett revisited Scotland after an absence of sixteen years. He came back to Glasgow, where he met Dr. Moore, and other old acquaintances, to enjoy what Sir Arthur Helps, with more than his customary liveliness, has described as the greatest good of success, namely, the pleasure of convincing friends and relations that one is not such a fool as one was once supposed to be. His mother was still alive, and no longer in need of the help of the family at Bonhill. Her daughter's marriage had been a prosperous one; Mr. Telfer, the husband, had thriven in the world as a manufacturer, and had bought the small estate of Scotston in Peebleshire. Mrs. Smollett was now living with her daughter, and it was here that her son came to visit her.

A story given to Dr. Moore by one of the family, which on the whole proves that one branch of the Smolletts at least had a taste for somewhat untimely practical jokes, tells how the novelist was presented to his mother by Mrs. Telfer as a gentleman from the West Indies who had known her son. Smollett entered into the spirit of the jest till the comedy of the situation was too much for him, and he smiled. Then his mother recognized him at once. "She immediately sprung from her chair, and throwing her arms around his neck, exclaimed, 'Ah, my son! my son! I have found you at last.' She afterwards told him," Dr. Moore goes on, "that if he had kept his austere look, and continued to *gloom*, he might have escaped detection some time longer; 'but your old roguish smile,' added she, 'betrayed you at once.'" Smollett may, as the biographer asserts, and as passages in "Humphrey Clinker" go to prove, have been endowed "with some share of that affectionate prejudice in favour of his relations and countrymen, of which the natives of Scotland are accused by their philosophic neighbours," but he must certainly have kept his sentimental emotions in good order to be able to play this little farce.

The second interruption arose directly out of *The Critical Review*, and it came upon Smollett in 1759. The review had been started in '56, in opposition to the *Monthly*. The capital seems to have been found by Mr. Hamilton, the printer, one of the young Edinburgh men who had reasons of a very sufficient kind for escaping hurriedly from the " proodfu toon " immediately after the hanging of Captain Porteous. Hamilton had become a prosperous man, and he saw an opportunity of doing a good stroke of business in opposition to Griffiths, the owner of the *Monthly*. The enterprise was one which has been often copied in the history of " the trade," and indeed had its precedents even in 1756. It was the story of *The Spectator* and *The Examiner* over again, with variations, and was a sketch, as it were, of *The Edinburgh* and *The Quarterly* battle, of the rivalry of Constable and Murray, and of Bacon's fight with Bungay. *The Critical Review*, like some successors in fiction, and in reality, was announced to be written by "gentlemen for gentlemen,"—by a " Society of Gentlemen," to quote the exact words of the title-page. The review brought Smollett an ample share of disputes with gentlemen who thought themselves unfairly treated, and in some cases considered it an aggravation of the wrong that they were criticized by Scotchmen. Grainger was made furious by a notice—a scoffing notice—of his Tibullus, and Churchill fell furiously foul of the review because it did not praise the Rosciad. These things, however, may be said to belong to Smollett's literary life. The worst trouble into which he was led by *The Critical Review* was with an old acquaintance who was not by profession a writing man, but who had thought fit to rush into print in defence of himself.

Captain Knowles had commanded the *Weymouth*, of sixty guns, in Vernon's West Indian fleet. Whether he sat among others for Captain Oakum does not appear, but it is perhaps worth noting that he took part in the barren action with the French ships on the coast of Hispaniola, described in "Roderick Random," and that his name is not mentioned with praise in Smollett's account of the expedition to Carthagena. He had continued in the service, and in 1757 was a rear-admiral, flying his flag as second in command, under Sir Edward Hawke, in the Channel. Though he had never absolutely failed, his reputation was not good. Walpole describes him as "a vain man of more parade than real bravery." In 1757, he was engaged under Hawke to command the squadron in the Basque Roads, in the attack on Rochefort. There were good officers of both services engaged in the affair —Conway, Cornwallis, and Wolfe among the soldiers, and Howe, Knowles's second in command, among the seamen. Unfortunately, Knowles, who was entrusted with the actual direction of the operations by Hawke, and Sir John Mordaunt the general, were not up to their work, and the co-operation ended as co-operations have not uncommonly done, in differences of opinion, undecided action, and a council of war, which, as a matter of course, resolved to do nothing. There was an angry outcry in the country, and Admiral Knowles came in for his share of blame. A Court of Inquiry was held, and though he was not condemned for actual misconduct, he was certainly accused by implication of having behaved with little ability or enterprise. The Admiral would not sit quiet under this tacit condemnation. He published a pamphlet to defend himself, which came to *The Critical Review*, and was duly commented on by Smollett himself.

The article which brought this woe on Smollett may be quoted at length, not only as a specimen of the journalistic style of the time, which, as the reader will observe, does not differ for the worse from our own, but as an example of what a rear-admiral and a British jury thought intolerably severe criticism in 1758. It is also not long, which is a merit:

"The design of this pamphlet is to vindicate Admiral Knowles from an implicated charge contained in the report of the Board of Inquiry concerning the last expedition to the coast of France. It is there said, that the design of attacking Fort Fouras was laid aside upon the representations of Vice-Admiral Knowles that the ship intended for that service was on ground at the distance of four or five miles from the shore. Mr. Knowles has, in our opinion, proved that this ship was actually on shore, as were also the bomb-ketches and the *Coventry* frigate. It likewise plainly appears that one of these bomb-ketches was actually conducted by the pilot Thierry ; that the master of the *Barfleur* sounded the river Charente from bank to bank ; and that the service was retarded but

9

three hours by Thierry's being sent to chase in the *Magnanime*.

" He has given us some reasons (though to us not satis-factory) for the fort being built on the shore without gun-shot of the Channel ; he labours hard to prove that the Fort Fouras was inaccessible by sea, and with respect to the report of Captain Colby's offering to carry in the *Princess Amelia*, he says it is a mystery that may be unriddled by a monosyllable, that may be guessed at without explanation. But, after all these demonstrations, we find that no person sounded nearer than three-quarters of a mile of the fort ; and whether the Channel was not within the distance is still a point far from being ascertained. In the name of Heaven ! why was all this space left untried ? If the persons employed on this service were afraid of approaching nearer the fort in the day, they might have, with great safety, executed the de-sign in the night. They might have foreseen their omission, in this particular, would leave the most material point undecided, and consequently subject them to doubts, suspicion, and censure. The most valuable part of this pamphlet is the affixed carte (*sic*) of the road of Basque with the different soundings of the coast marked by figures."

Modern generals have had to put up with much worse than this from correspondents actually in the camp; but in 1758, officers were not yet case hardened, and Admiral Knowles brought an action for libel against *The Review*. It is plain that Smollett, and his publishers, were by no means sure of the result of a trial. Perhaps they

thought the jury would be of opinion that they had
gone too far in practically reaffirming a charge which had
not been considered as proved by the Court of Inquiry.
It must not be forgotten that the press had not yet
established its claim to immunity in the criticism of
public men as fully as it did later on. Whatever his
motive may have been, Smollett made an attempt to
avoid an action by the use of private interest. He
appealed to Wilkes, who was himself destined to fight a
battle for the independence of the press at no distant
date. A few days after he had written asking for the
help of the future demagogue on behalf of Dr. Johnson's
servant, he made this appeal for himself.

"Chelsea, *March* 24, 1759.

"Dear Sir,—*Ecce iterum Crispinus!* Your generosity with respect to Johnson shall be the theme of our
applause and thanksgiving. I shall be very proud to
find myself comprehended in your league offensive and
defensive, nay, I consider myself already as a contracting
party, and have recourse to the assistance of my allies.
It is not, I believe, unknown to you that Admiral
Knowles has taken exception at a paragraph in *The
Critical Review* of last May, and commenced a prosecution against the printer. Now whatever termination the
trial may have, we shall infallibly be exposed to a considerable expense ; and therefore I wish to see the prosecution quashed. Some gentlemen, who are my friends,
have undertaken to find out, and talk with those who
are supposed to have influence with the said Admiral;
may I beg the same favour of you? The trial will come

on in the beginning of May : and if the affair cannot be compromised, we intend to kick up a dust, and die hard.   In a word, if that foolish Admiral has any respect to his own character, he will be quiet, rather than provoke further the resentment of,

> " Dear sir,
>
> "Your very obliged humble servant,
>
> " T. SMOLLETT."

If Admiral Knowles heard of the menace at the end of this letter, he may be pardoned for refusing to yield to what looks at least very like an attempt to bully by threats of other and worse personal attacks in the future.   His later conduct, if truly reported, is, however, sufficient evidence that he cannot have acted on motives of a magnanimous kind.   According to Dr. Moore's account, the Admiral's counsel declared in the Court of King's Bench that his client had no wish to punish a wretched printer, " but to discover who had written the offensive article," and " that when he (viz., the Admiral) should come to the knowledge of the author, if he proved to be a gentleman, another kind of satisfaction would be demanded of him."   A barrister was assuredly strangely employed in delivering what was practically a challenge in open court, and it may be that Dr. Moore is wrong as to the details of the story.   In some way or other Smollett was made to understand that the Admiral was prepared to accept the satisfaction of a gentleman.   He at once took the course which might have been expected of him.   Smollett may have been quarrelsome, and occasionally even insolent, but he had the qualities of his defects.

He was not the man to skulk behind a printer, and he came forward at once; whereupon the Admiral brought an action against him personally, and got him sentenced to a fine of £100, and three months' imprisonment in the King's Bench prison. The needful comment upon this most unseamanlike and unsportsmanlike behaviour on the Admiral's part has been made by Sir Walter Scott, who himself, when threatened with a challenge by General Gourgaud, was cheerfully prepared to shoot his man with the pistols which had once belonged to the General's old master, Napoleon. "How the Admiral," says Sir Walter, "reconciled his conduct to the rules usually observed by gentlemen, we are not informed; but the proceeding seems to justify even Smollett's strength of expression, when he terms him an officer without resolution, and a man without veracity." Admiral Knowles seems decidedly to have belonged to the class of naval officers who had to be "encouraged" by the shooting of Byng.

Smollett did his three months and paid his fine. Imprisonment in the King's Bench prison had its compensations. Gentlemen confined there were treated (as long as they could pay their fees) on the footing of State prisoners. They had their rooms, could receive visitors, and do their work if they had any to do. Smollett does not seem to have had any difficulty in finding money to meet the expenses brought upon him by the trial. Except indeed during one period of his life, before and after the translation of "Don Quixote," he does not appear ever to have been in serious difficulties, and then they were partly caused by the failure of somebody in the West

Indies, who owed money to Mrs. Smollett, and to his own
generosity in helping a friend.   He gave his help in the
form of a promissory note, like a good Scotchman.   There
is something irresistibly attractive it seems to the Scotch
mind in the act of signing a bill.   Sir Walter Scott
observed, and also proved by his own example, that a
Scotchman who will think twice before parting with half-
a-crown of ready money, will make himself liable for
hundreds of pounds of paper quite gaily.   Once at least
in his life Smollett's blood was too much for him, and he
suffered for being a Scotchman.   The period of financial
distress seems to have lasted from 1753 to 1756, and in
the course of it, Smollett was at times hard pressed.   He
had to borrow money from his wife's relations, and his
own friends, till remittances came in from the West Indies,
and earnings were attained to in London.   In '53 his need
was so great that he was compelled to cash a bill for fifty
guineas at a month's date which he was allowed to draw
on Provost Drummond, at a discount of £2 12s. 6d., for
the month.   The money was due for editorial work done
for the Provost's brother, who had written a book, and
wanted it revised.   Provost Drummond was plainly
another good Scotchman, for it can only have been an
artistic love of a bill which prevented him from agreeing
to pay at call.   Continued delays in the remittances from
the West Indies, and the difficulty of making money in
London, kept Smollett under the necessity of appealing
to his brother-in-law, Mr. Telfer, or to his friend Dr.
Macaulay, until the appearance of *The Critical Review*
in 1756.   In 1754 the difficulties of the day were
aggravated by an unpleasant adventure of a not un-

common kind in the eighteenth century : Smollett was robbed of his watch and purse, in " the stage coach between Chelsea and London," by some gentleman of the road, of the stamp of his own Rifle. After 1756, however, he seems to have attained to a regular income. He was able to meet the costs of Admiral Knowles' action, and to travel to Scotland and abroad, and to find the necessary money himself. To some extent his comparative prosperity may have been due to good fortune in securing a solvent tenant for Mrs. Smollett's West Indian property. In a letter written to an American correspondent in 1763, just before he left England, he speaks of himself as enjoying, in right of his wife, " a comfortable tho' moderate estate in Jamaica." But the bulk of his income must have come from his own work. According to the bad custom of the time, he had been paid for the translation of " Don Quixote " before the work was done, and as an inevitable consequence the task had to be toiled through in the midst of money trouble. Later on, however, Smollett seems to have been able to avoid the pitfall of payment in advance. The sums which he actually received cannot have been insignificant. The actual money paid for the history is said to have been, first and last, £2,000, which was as good, all things considered, as twice the sum would be now. When the eighteenth century is spoken of as a time in which men of letters were very badly paid, and the reading public small (and these rather self-righteous assertions turn up every now and then), it is well to remember that books on a large scale were often fairly well paid for, and that the bookseller seems to have been able to rely on a purchasing public for them with a confidence which his successor, the publisher, does not seem often able to feel.

No portion of the writing which Smollett did during these years belongs to the living part of his work. The great history helped, no doubt, to gain him his right to the adjectives "learned and ingenious" before his name in his own time, but it can hardly be said to have survived as part of the historical literature of the country. It was a considerable feat to write four quartos, founded on the consultation of three hundred books, in fourteen months. Speaking roughly, the feat was equivalent, in mere writing, to two full leading articles a day, done for a year and two months right on without a break. When it is remembered that this was done in addition to the monthly labour for *The Critical Review*, of which Smollett seems to have written the greater part, during the early years at least, it is not surprising that he should have been unable to leave his house, and have ruined his health by incessant application to the desk. Nothing can be more honourable than this work as a piece of honest labour, undertaken to pay off debts and win a position of independence; but from the literary point of view it was toil wasted. The result was, and could only be, journalism, which, from the very nature of it, is not "a thing immortal," but, on the contrary, a thing fit for immediate consumption. No man who was meant by nature to be an historian would undertake to read up and write a history of England on any scale, still less in four volumes quarto, in fourteen months. In this generation no writer of anything approaching Smollett's standing would, for very conscience' sake, undertake the task for ten times the pay, even if he could get it. But in the middle of the last century, there seems to have been a belief that the good workman was fit for all work, and as the booksellers saw that the public would buy history, they made their arrangements accordingly. Smollett wrote history as Goldsmith did, though on a larger scale, as part of the day's work. Whoever will turn to his history without expecting more than he ought to expect, will find a well-written narrative, belonging, for the most part, to the same order of work as the summaries of the year printed by some newspapers, only decidedly better done than such things usually are. Smollett himself took it very seriously, and assured Dr. Moore, with almost touching earnestness, that he had written " without espousing any faction." The words which follow are too good to be left unquoted : " though," he goes on, " I own I sat down to write with a warm side to those principles in which I was educated ; but in the course of my inquiries some of the Whig ministers turned out such a set of sordid knaves, that I could not help stigmatizing them for their want of integrity and sentiment." The study of history had produced on Smollett's mind what some will think is its proper effect. It had made him a good sound Tory. But has not Smollett's position as an historian been summed up by Mr. Thackeray ? " Once when Mr. Crawley asked what the young people were reading, the governess replied ' Smollett.' 'Oh, Smollett,' said Mr. Crawley, quite satisfied. ' His history is more dull, but by no means so dangerous as that of Mr. Hume. It is history you are reading ? ' ' Yes,' said Miss Rose; without, however, adding that it was the history of Mr.

Humphrey Clinker." This is one of the many things
for which unprejudiced people love Miss Rebecca Sharpe.
" The Compendium of Voyages," " The Modern Universal History," and the rest, were openly done as honest
journeyman work for want of a better, and Smollett's
share in them must have been mainly confined to recruit-
ing, and exercising a paternal control over, the workmen
whom Mr. Jerry Melford met at his house in Chelsea.

The translations belong to a higher order. For a man
who loved Cervantes and Le Sage so well as Smollett did,
it must have been a pleasure to live with them, and his
versions of their masterpieces would necessarily have the
merit of work that is done with zest. As regards the
Spaniard, Smollett had the usual fate of translators of
"Don Quixote." "A gentleman from the country"
wrote to point out he did not know the language well
enough, and had come to "grief and breakage" over
that notorious stumbling-block "duelos y quebrantos,"
and other rough places. The critic, however, was as
much at sea as the translator, and as all men were till
Diego Clemencin came and made the rough places smooth.
Smollett shows no sign of ignorance of Spanish ; indeed
he had ample time to learn it between the date of payment
for his translation and the actual doing of it, and his
faults were not of a kind which knowledge of the language
would have saved him from. When he goes wrong, it is
generally not because he does not understand the original,
but because he chooses to add to its meaning. He had
a tendency to abound in the sense of his author, to force
the note, and heighten the colour, which could at times
produce a degree of falsity nearly equal to downright

mistranslation. Take, for example, the very first sentence of "Don Quixote," which is not only convenient but good as a text. Cervantes says, "In a village of La Mancha, whereof I do not care to remember the name, there lived not long ago one of those gentlemen who have a lance on the rack, an old-fashioned buckler, a lean hackney, and a coursing greyhound." In Smollett this becomes, "In a certain corner of La Mancha, the name of which I do not choose to remember, there lately lived one of those country gentlemen who adorn their halls with a rusty lance and worm-eaten target, and ride forth on the skeleton of a horse, to course with a sort of starved greyhound." Obviously one half of this is pure surplusage, mere useless insistance on the author's meaning. Some of this padding may be due to mere haste, since it is far easier to use many words than few in translations as elsewhere; but much of it must also have been deliberately put in with the object of giving the spirit of the author. The attempt was frequently doomed to failure. In the course of this amplification and ex-aggeration the flavour of the original is lost. There is, however, this much to be said for Smollett's translation, that he was sufficiently in sympathy with Cervantes to exaggerate on his lines, and the translation has an original literary value of its own. He treated Cervantes somewhat as Urquhart treated Rabelais; but in the opinion of competent judges, Urquhart's "Rabelais" is no mean feat in literature.

There is a difficulty in the way of all criticism of the value of the other translations which pass under Smollett's name, and for which he is nominally answerable—and it is the difficulty of knowing how much of them he did himself, and how much of them was done for him by workmen of the stamp of those he used to meet at Farmer's Coffee House. Even in his own time, the "Gil Blas" was spoken of as "passing under his name," and it is now confidently attributed to another hand. As regards the "Complete Works of M. de Voltaire," we have his own word, in the letter to an American friend already quoted, that he did only a very small part of it, over and above the historical and critical notes. Within the last few months, the translation of "Candide" given in the "Complete Works"—of both the parts, the first which no son of Adam but Voltaire could possibly have written, and the second which he allowed to pass under his name, but which cannot be his—has been reprinted in a Bowdlerized form by Professor Morley in The Universal Library. This version is so spirited that the temptation to attribute it to Smollett is great. That he took hints for some of the nastiest passages in the "Adventures of an Atom" from the very un-Voltairian second part is not to be doubted. But this is no proof that he did the translation, and it is unlikely that he would have failed to claim such an important piece of work as a version of "Candide," if he had really been its author. On the other hand, he did claim the "Gil Blas" which is disputed. Judging by internal evidence (the only really satisfactory test when direct evidence is wanting), I am inclined to think that he cannot have done the "Candide." It does not seem to me to have the notes of the undoubted translation of "Don Quixote," the continual exaggeration and forcing of the tone which make Smollett's English such a swollen version of the Spanish of

Cervantes. On the whole, Smollett appears to have done most of this part of his work by contract. He hired a gang of literary workmen, and supervised them. In the literary world of his time he would have no difficulty in finding a number of good hands who would do very well under intelligent supervision.

While Admiral Knowles' action was hanging over his head, Smollett was inclined to grumble at *The Critical Review*, and expresses a rather ungrateful wish that he could hang his pen up for good, and be done with praise and blame. Yet it might be plausibly argued that by much the most really important work which Smollett did between "Peregrine Pickle," and "Humphrey Clinker," was done for *The Critical Review.* It is true that nobody can now-a-days be expected to read the two hundred volumes of this magazine, or even that part of them to which Smollett contributed; but then who reads "The Reprisal," or "Sir Launcelot Greaves," or at least who reads them twice? *The Critical Review* had a place of some importance in the history of English journalism. It was a distinct effort at least to establish a scholarly literary magazine which should not be written, like Griffiths' *Monthly*, by hack writers resident in a bookseller's garret, but by a "society of gentlemen," who could boast of some pretensions to a position of independence. The magazine looks poor and rather crude alongside of its modern successors. It would be rash to make a general statement as to the contents of the whole two hundred volumes, and the biographer of Smollett is not bound to take note of them beyond the year 1760 or thereabouts. Possibly enough there may be longer and more elaborate work hidden away some-

where in this heap of volumes, but as a rule, and certainly
in the earlier years, *The Critical Review* consisted almost
wholly of short notices of books, such as are now printed
under a heading of "recent publications," or "the editor's
table," or some such thing.   Speaking from a knowledge
which does not profess to be more than superficial, I
should feel inclined to say that this work was done, at
least during Smollett's editorship, with considerable spirit.

As for the fairness, that was a matter of opinion at the
time, and can hardly be estimated now.   The books
reviewed have been in so many cases hopelessly forgotten,
and it is impossible to check the reviewer even if one
wished to do so.   "*The Critical* reviewers I believe,'
said Doctor Johnson, "often review without reading the
books through ; but lay hold of a topic and write chiefly
from their own minds."   The practice is one which, if all
tales be true, has not passed away with *The Critical Review.*
Naturally the author and the critic take very different
views of its legitimacy.   The latter perhaps justifies himself by the excuse for this custom of indolent irrespon-
sible reviewing implied in Johnson's criticism on the
rival of *The Critical*—" *The Monthly* reviewers are duller
men, and are glad to read the book through."   During
Smollett's rule at least *The Critical Review* was not dull,
and if it did not contain much criticism of permanent
value, at least it supplied its readers with some smart talk
about the books and the topics of the day, and helped to
popularize literary things.   In this respect Smollett's work
for it was very similar to his history, which was undoubtedly written to meet a popular demand, and was
republished in a second edition in parts, and with plates

executed by Strange, obviously in order that it might be put within the reach of the most modest purse. As a book-seller's speculation it seems to have been highly successful. Twelve thousand numbers was the average of the sale, and it may be doubted, whether even in these days, with a larger purchasing public, and when paper is cheaper, though certainly not so good, and when steam has made it possible to print on a larger scale at a much more moderate rate, such a work could either be sold for less, or relied upon to find so good a sale.

Smollett's connection with *The British* was confined to the contribution of "Sir Launcelot Greaves." It is hardly a far-fetched supposition that Smollett's residence in the King's Bench prison suggested to him the unfortunate scheme of reviving "Don Quixote and his Squire" in the England of the eighteenth century. He also may have wished to produce a work in a prison, "which is the seat of inconvenience and the habitation of every dismal sound." It was certainly a most ill-advised attempt. Whatever chance "Sir Launcelot Greaves" may have had of being a good story, was ruined by the lumbering and hope-lessly unmanageable machinery Smollett chose to adopt in a spirit of unintelligent imitation. There are flashes of the old fire of "Roderick Random" in "Sir Launce-lot." Whenever Smollett is dealing with picaresque adventure, or is pillorying an enemy, he is still alive. Sir Launcelot Greaves is himself a fine fellow. The sailor, Captain Crewe, and his nephew, the attorney, have also some of the old vitality. But the story as a whole is crushed by the comparison with "Don Quixote," which Smollett forced on his reader. He was himself conscious of his mistake, and after apologizing for ıt, if that can be called an apology which was, in fact, an expression of high contempt for carping critics, he dropped the parody of the Don and Sancho, and gave himself up freely to make sketches of rogues and of madmen. But it was too late, and "Sir Launcelot Greaves" was doomed to remain an unsuccessful copy of the mere outside of Cervantes' novel, redeemed here and there by scenes which prove that Smollett had not yet lost his old verve, and might yet do work as original, and as much his own, as "Roderick Random" or "Peregrine Pickle."

The "Reprisal," which appeared in 1757, stands alone in two respects in Smollett's life. It was his only successful attempt to reach the stage, and it led to the soldering up of an old quarrel. The plot of this two-act comedy may have given Marryat the first idea of "The Three Cutters," and is worked up with no small liveliness. Its characters have a distinct comic *vis* of a rather broad kind. The sailors Lyon, Haulyard, and Block, are good as Smollett's sailors always were; Oclabber and Maclaymore, the exiled Jacobites in the French service, are first drafts of the immortal Lismahago. Like most of Smollett's work in those years, this comedy has its touch of journalism. It was written to revive the patriotic sentiment of the nation, which had been much depressed by Byng's failure off Minorca, and the consequent loss of the island in the previous year. The *actualité* of the subject may have helped to persuade Garrick to accept the piece for Drury Lane; but he would have been a less sagacious man than he was if he had not seen that the editor of *The Critical Review* was entitled to more consideration than the unknown author of the "Regicide." He certainly behaved handsomely in the matter by acting the part of Zara on the first night to draw a good house, and then contributing twenty pounds out of his own pocket to increase the author's profits. Smollett did penance for Marmozet by writing the great actor a most grateful letter, and then repaid the service by praising him most heartily in *The Critical Review*—for the wicked practice of "log-rolling" was already known, though not yet named. Smollett rolled logs himself, and for himself, in the most gallant fashion. *The Critical Review* praised him, and he praised his friends in *The Critical Review*. When, as was the case with the author of "Douglas," one of the editor's friends was by accident "slated," or even not sufficiently praised, Smollett hastened to explain that it was an oversight, and would not have happened if he had been on the spot to prevent it. One would hardly state the immoral proposition that one's friends were to be "cracked up accordingly," with more audacity.

CHAPTER VII.

BEFORE Smollett left England in 1763, he had gone through what must have been the most unpleasant experience of his career. From May '62 to February '63 was for him a period of political journalism, the first and the last in his life. In an evil hour he undertook to edit *The Briton*, a weekly paper in support of Bute's administration. There is no reason to suppose that Smollett did not enter on the fight with perfect honesty. It is true that he dedicated his " History " to the great Pitt, and that he had praised him in public, and equally true that he afterwards attacked him with unmeasured ferocity in the " Adventures of an Atom." Nothing, I think, not even disappointment, disease, and a *systema nervosum maxime irritabile*, can justify the tone of that political satire; but Smollett might well have reconciled a belief in the Minister's personal greatness with a conviction that the war had been carried on long enough for the interest of the country, and that it was now time to make peace. If he also thought that enough English money had gone to help Frederick of Prussia in his fight with the House of Austria, and that the sooner we cut ourselves adrift from the wars of the Continent the better, he was in agreement with many

Englishmen, and might have cited not a little of Pitt's own eloquence in early years in support of his views. Unfortunately honesty of conviction is not enough to make successful journalism ; ability even will hardly do it. There must be a cause to fight for, and leaders who will head the fight. Bute, however, and the king, though they had a cause, and a very fair one, contrived to ruin it effectually by their own backstairs intrigue. They condemned their supporters to fight what must in any case have been an uphill battle, under particularly disadvantageous circumstances. Then, when they had done their best, Bute left them in the lurch. The history of *The Briton* is figuratively told, in the " Adventures of an Atom," in a passage which may be quoted with suppressions. Mr. Orator Taycho [Pitt] takes the field, and then Yak-strot [Bute] " began to put himself in a posture of defence. He hired a body of mercenaries, and provided some dirtmen and rhymers. Then, taking the field, a sharp contest and pelting match ensued, but the dispute was soon terminated. Yak-strot's versifiers turned out no great conjurers on the trial." (Here follows a description of the pelting match, which may be read in the original.) "Yak-strot having suffered wofully in his own person, and seeing his partizans in confusion, thought proper to retreat. Yet although discomfited he was not discouraged. On the contrary, having at bottom a fund of fanaticism, which, like camomile, grows the faster for being trod upon, he became more obstinately bent than ever upon prosecuting his own schemes for the good of the people in their own despite. His vanity was likewise buoyed up by the flattery of his creatures, who extolled the passive courage he had shown in the late engagement. Though every part of him still tingled and stunk from the balls of the enemy, he persuaded himself that not one of their missiles had taken place ; and of consequence that there was something of divinity in his person. Full of this notion he discarded his rhymers and his dirt-casters as unnecessary, and resolved to bear the brunt of the battle in his own individual."

In other words, Bute had become convinced, before the year was out, that the only effect of *The Briton* was to draw more attacks upon him. The failure must have been cruelly humiliating to Smollett. He was not the man to take kindly to figuring on the beaten side. He had quarrelled, as a necessary consequence of his activity as Bute's supporter, with Wilkes. The good-natured demagogue was, for his part, quite prepared to go through the battle of dirt-throwing with good humour, but Smollett was too much in earnest to imitate his example. He attacked his old friend in unmeasured terms. Naturally he was himself very roughly handled by Wilkes and his men, and Smollett's sensitiveness to personal attack was in exact proportion to his readiness to attack others. When *The Briton* was given up, he was stung, aggravated, and humiliated beyond endurance. His sense of his personal importance had been horribly shocked. The emotions of this year of conflict, and the disappointment which came at the end of it, acted with killing force on his enfeebled health. Early in 1763, the death of his daughter and only child gave him a final blow, and in the following June he left England accompanied by Mrs. Smollett, and two young ladies who were put under their care, and sought for peace and health in the south of Europe.

He stayed abroad from the June of '63 till the early spring of '65. The history of this period of exile has been told by himself in those "Travels through France and Italy" which, justly enough, excited the ridicule of Sterne. They are certainly dreary reading. Smollett went abroad in a frame of mind sufficiently clearly described by himself. He looked upon himself as a man "traduced by malice, persecuted by faction, abandoned by false patrons;" and, however much this view may have been coloured by his own atrabilious frame of mind, there was no doubt absolute truth in the following words, which describe him as "overwhelmed by the sense of a domestic calamity which it was not in the power of fortune to repair." It was not until shortly before his return to England, that rest, and the climate of Northern Italy, began to restore him to some measure of health and peace of mind.

His view of what he saw of France and Italy is naturally darkened by his own sufferings, and the book in which he described his experiences is full of melancholy details of the state of his health, and dreary stories of the extortion of landlords and the insolence of postilions. Almost the only parts of it which flash up into any tolerable degree of vitality, are those very heterodox opinions on works of art, for which the learned Smelfungus was laughed at by the author of the "Sentimental Journey." Some of them do not look nearly so heterodox now as they did in 1766. There are probably a good few persons who would not feel themselves conscious of guilt if they expressed very much

the same opinion as Smollett's on the famous Venus at
Florence. On the whole, these judgments on works of
art, which Smollett introduces with a disclaimer of any
pretensions to the title of judge, show a certain hard sense
which is not without its attractions. At least they are
considerably more honest, and incomparably more critical,
than the routine admiration of people who get into
ecstasies because they think it is the right thing to do.
Smollett looked at these marvels for himself, and
when he did not feel any spontaneous admiration, he said
so. His independence is the more respectable because
there is not a trace in him of that flippant and ignorant
contempt for things which they have neither the training
nor the capacity to understand, which certain so-called
humourists think fit to display with ostentation in our
time.

After his return to England, Smollett does not seem to
have lived much in London ; he was barely three years
in his native country before his health compelled him to
fly back to Northern Italy. During that period he resided
for a time at Bath, which had always been a favourite
haunt of his, and he paid one long and last visit to Scotland. In the midst of these movements he still pushed
on with his work ; he published his travels, he wrote the
continuation of his history down to the year 1762, which
is generally bound up with Hume's, and just before leaving
England he published the " Adventures of an Atom."
This work, for which he undoubtedly got some hints from
the spurious second part of " Candide," is that part of all
his writing which could best be spared. Except in certain
parts of Swift, there is nothing, at least in the productions

of any writer of a high rank, to surpass the mere animal nastiness of this satire. From first to last Smollett rings the changes on the words dirt, sores, filth, evacuations up and down, till he produces an intolerable feeling of disgust, not at the things and persons he meant to deride, but at himself. Then, too, the satire is so utterly indiscriminate. Not only are George II., the Duke of Cumberland, and the Duke of Newcastle bespattered with nastiness, but the same treatment is meted out to Anson,. Mansfield, and, above all, to Pitt. It is impossible not to feel the vigour with which this rather ignoble work is done; and certain passages haunt the mind like the memory of something odious and cruel one has seen by accident, and in the streets. The best that can be said for it is that it seems to have cleared Smollett's bosom of much perilous stuff. It was a poorness in him to unpack his heart with curses, but at least he did it once and for all; when he took his pen up again in exile, and in full view of death, it was to write with a kindlier humanity than he had ever shown before.

The good done to Smollett's health by the first visit to Italy had been very temporary. Shortly after his return to England, he had begun to suffer from insomnia. A visit to Scotland in 1766 gave him some relief, but his constitution was irretrievably ruined, and two years later he was under the necessity of leaving England for ever. He attempted to secure the post of Consul, and applied to Hume, who was at that time Under Secretary of State, to help him in his application. Hume, with his usual good nature, did his best with Lord Shelburne, but it was to no purpose. The consulates at Nice and Leg

horn were already disposed of, and Smollett was compelled to go abroad relying entirely on his own resources.
He left England at the end of 1768, and made his way
by Lucca and Pisa to Leghorn. Here he settled at the
village of Monte Novo, where he remained until his
death in 1771. His work followed him to Italy; at
Lucca and at Pisa he was engaged in finishing up what
editing was still due to the "Modern Universal History."
This seems to have been the last piece of mere business
industry he did. At Leghorn he was engaged on
"Humphrey Clinker," which appeared in 1771, in the
very year of his death.

Sir Walter Scott has called "The Expedition of Humphrey Clinker," "the last, and like music sweetest
in the close, the most pleasing" of the works of
Smollett. The description is not only true, but short
of the truth. "Humphrey Clinker" is not only, by
general consent, the best of Smollett's works, but
it has a manifold superiority to anything else he did
in the course of his literary life. If his life had ended
before it was written, he would still have been a considerable figure in the literature of his time, and have
exercised a decided influence on his contemporaries.
He would have been admired by Doctor Carlyle, and
his society would have been sought by men whose
friendship was an honour. Robertson and Hume would
have been proud to recognize him as a countryman
and fellow-man of letters. The "Adventures of a
Guinea" would have equally been written by his pupil
Johnson. But without "Humphrey Clinker," Smollett
would not have been distinctly and undeniably one of

the first humourists of the eighteenth century, and still less would the tenderness, which lay under all the fierceness of his disposition, have been made so manifest. His own description of Lord Bute as a man with "a fund of fanaticism which, like camomile, grows the faster for being trod on," invites the application to himself, in an infinitely more honourable way, of a famous sentence in Bacon's essay " Of Adversity : " "certainly Virtue is like precious Odours, most fragrant when they are incensed or crushed; for *Prosperity* doth best discover Vice, but *Adversity* doth best discover Virtue." Toil, disappointment, suffering, and domestic calamity had tamed and disciplined the ferocity out of Smollett before he sat down to work at " Humphrey Clinker." He was still the same man. He had not lost his fondness for speaking of certain physical facts, and even for dwelling on them. He still introduced individuals, and fought out private quarrels, even in the last of his books. The picture of the ungrateful Nabob at Bath and his benefactor, Mr. Serle, is supposed, apparently on good evidence, to be Smollett's revenge for the ungrateful behaviour of a man whom he had once befriended; but if he was the same Smollett, it was with a difference. There is an atmosphere of kindliness in " Humphrey Clinker " peculiar to this alone among his works. It leaves no bitter taste in the mouth. The intention to make vice hateful by dwelling only on vice, which renders his earlier works such one-sided pictures of life, is absent here. He seems to have been glad to be done with rogues, and even with fools, and to have wished at the end of his warfare on earth to live for a time with people who might be laughable, but were never to be wholly hateful. Even Tabitha Bramble, old cat as she is, is a pardonable old cat. One has a general impression that if the Lieutenant in H. M.'s navy, who fell so untimely in action with the French frigate, had not lost the number of his mess on that occasion, Tabitha would not have been the Vixen whom it required all Lieutenant Lismahago's courage to tackle. As for the others, there is not one of them we would not have liked to have met. Miss Lydia Melford is a somewhat shadowy young lady, but on further acquaintance, she would no doubt have been found to be a very charming girl. The still more shadowy Wilson was doubtless much to be envied. As for Mr. Jerry Melford, he was a very fine young fellow, a very gallant young gentleman indeed, and when he bullied his sister, it was all out of pure brotherly love and desire for her good. Even the impersonal things—the Methodist craze, for example—are kindly treated. Smollett was Scotchman enough not to share Fielding's dislike of a movement which damaged the Church of England, but he had a great deal of the eighteenth-century dislike and distrust of fanaticism. He would certainly not in earlier years have preferred to dwell on whatever was good in Methodism, as he does in " Humphrey Clinker."

Because of this very humanity, because he was not intent on rousing the generous indignation of his reader with the sordid and vicious disposition of the world, because it may almost be said Smollett had gone back, at the end of his life, to the spirit of Le Sage, after beginning it by imitating his form, these characters of his have an unwonted human reality. Beneath all their oddities

and their external crust of eccentricy, there is a living
personality. They are, none of them, altogether good,
any more than they are altogether bad. Matthew Bramble
shows himself in the course of his "lamentations" as
probably the most credible specimen of the *bourreau
bienfaisant* in literature. Poor Tabitha is not only the
soured old maid of comedy, but a human being with a
distinct character of her own. There is something to be
said even for her unconscionable use of her brother's
poultry yard and his flocks and herds. Even the affection
she lavishes on that insufferable brute Chowder, only went
that bad road for want of a better. She schemes and
scolds and is frightened when Matthew does at last rebel
in a very individual way. No old maid was ever quite
like that, except Tabitha Bramble. Winifred Jenkins is
not all misspelling and servant-maid gossip. Humphrey
Clinker, though he gives his name to the book, is comparatively colourless, but even he leaves a distinct
impression of good and honest simplicity. The flower of
the book is beyond all question Lismahago. Until Rett-
meister Dugald Dalgetty came to stand by his side, the
lieutenant was unique ; even now he is very much a
"thing in itself." His pedantry, his prickly pride, his
firm conviction that he was an ill-used man, combined with
an almost ferocious determination to accept nobody's
pity, his stern economy, and his perfect readiness to be
lavish on what he thought a proper occasion, are all
individual traits consistent with one another, blended
together to make an absolutely credible character. Then,
too, Lismahago is an undoubted Scotchman ; no man of
any other race could have been quite so fond of a good

wrangle, or have defended a paradox with such tough
dexterity.   His family pride too is very Scotch, and so is
the unconscious contradiction between his contempt for
his brother's mechanical pursuits and his own perfect
readiness to attain to comfort by a mercenary marriage
with an unattractive old maid.   When he has attained to
this curious victory, and knows that for the rest of his life
he has got into tolerable quarters, it is delightful to see
how he expands in the sunshine of prosperity, and becomes almost frisky without ever losing his formidable
power of hitting hard on provocation, a power born in
him and developed in a life of war and wild adventure.
In whatever heaven the characters of novelists may attain
unto, one hopes that Lismahago and Lieutenant Thomas
Bowling may have met and discussed the fortunes of life
together.

The background of " Humphrey Clinker " differs from
the background of " Roderick Random " as the characters
of the last of Smollett's novels do from those of the first.
Bath and London are drawn again, but in quite another
spirit.   The testy comments of Matthew Bramble are
themselves modified by the goodness of heart of the
man himself.   Then alongside of his pictures, there are
always the views of Jerry Melford or even of Winifred
Jenkins.   The old man is bitter and disappointed, but
they in their several ways are full of youth and enjoyment.   They can revel heartily where he sees nothing but
the crush, and professes to feel nothing but the hot air,
and even less pleasant things which affect his nerves
and his nose.   Perhaps the most striking contrast between
the beginning and the end of Smollett's work is to be

traced between the Scotch scenes of "Roderick Random" and those of "Humphrey Clinker." Roderick seems only too happy to shake the dust of Scotland off his feet, and when he comes back to it, it is only to triumph and insult. In "Humphrey Clinker" Smollett dwells with a longing affection on the country of his fathers. He makes the *amende honorable* to the house at Bonhill for the pictures of the old judge and the young Actæon. Smollett had too good an eye for what was ridiculous, and still more for what was offensive, to spare his countrymen some wholesome ridicule where he thought it good for them. Swift himself could not have commented on certain unsanitary practices of the worthy people of Edinburgh in a more outspoken manner than Smollett. But these are only the wholesome corrections of a friend, and therefore, all the more likely to be effective. If servants in Edinburgh have not of later years been subjected to the inconveniences on which Winifred Jenkins commented, Smollett must have some of the credit. Even the rather sudden increase in the prevailing kindliness of the book which follows Matthew Bramble's entry into Scotland, is touching. Doctor Johnson himself would surely have pardoned a Scotchman for praise of Scotland written in disease and exile.

"Humphrey Clinker" appeared in time to shed some consolation on Smollett's deathbed. He was visited at Leghorn by his friend Doctor Armstrong, and he received some offices of courtesy from Sir Horace Mann; but disease must have confined him to his house, and have shut him off from society, even more completely than his multifarious occupations had done in London. The

weakness in his chest and the scorbutic illness of which
he has himself given such ample details, wore him
rapidly down. He met his death, as became him, with
perfect courage and even a certain grim jocularity. Not
long before the end came, he wrote to his friend and
countryman the famous John Hunter, " With respect
to myself I have nothing to say but that, if I can
prevail upon my wife to execute my last will, you shall
receive my poor carcase in a box after I am dead to be
placed among your rarities. I am already so dry and
emaciated, that I may pass for an Egyptian mummy,
without any other preparation than some pitch and
painted linen." There is some doubt as to the exact
date of his death, but it must have happened sometime
in September in 1771. He was only fifty-one years of
age. Like Fielding, he died comparatively young, and
lies buried in a foreign country. His grave is in the
old English cemetery at Leghorn, with the Mediterranean
to the west of him, as the ocean lies to the west of
Fielding at Oporto.

Two years after Smollett's death Professor Richardson,
who had been his friend, published at Glasgow the " Ode
to Independence," which was his only posthumous work,
unless the " prophetic passages," supposed to be extracted
from a letter written a few months before his death to
the Rev. Dr. —— of —— in Northumberland, and
published in 1795 in a " Dissertation on the Existence,
Nature, and Extent of the Prophetic Powers in the
Human Mind," are to be counted as genuine. Con-
sidering, however, that these passages predict the French
Revolution with considerable accuracy, they may safely

be classed with the more famous, and incomparably superior " Prophecy of Cazotte." The Ode may be read because it is the work of the creator of Lieutenants Bowling and Lismahago. It is the production of a vigorous workman, and if it is not poetry, at least Smollett was very much in earnest when he sang the offspring of Liberty and Disdain.

Had Smollett lived four years longer, he would have inherited the estate of Bonhill, which passed, on the death of his cousin James, to the children of his sister, Mrs. Telfer, who carried on the family name. It is a melancholy pendant to the history of Smollett's life, that his widow, who survived him for many years, was left in great poverty at Leghorn. The family of Bonhill appear to have done nothing for her. The estate in Jamaica had either been frittered away, or had ceased for some unknown reason to be productive. In 1783, Mr. Graham of Gartmore, and other admirers of her husband's, raised some money for her by a theatrical performance. The date of her death is unknown, but it is only too certain that the lady who was the original of Narcissa was reduced to subsist at last on the charity of strangers.

I have endeavoured to point out the literary quality of Smollett's work in the course of this book. To go back upon it now could only lead to repetition. Still in taking leave of one's man there is some profit in trying to place him—to use a convenient phrase. I cannot feel enough of the proper biographer's enthusiasm to profess a belief that I have been dealing—however inadequately— with one of the very great names of literature. It would not, I think, be possible to show that any great living force would have been wanting if Smollett had never written. He neither introduced a new moral element into the novel, as Richardson did, nor helped to perfect its form, as Fielding did. He was himself influenced by both of these men, and by a third also. It was not until he had read "Tristram Shandy" that he learned to make the humours of his characters uniformly kindly, and to see something else in eccentricity than material for rather hard fun. But a writer may have a place, and an honourable one in literature, although he has not been an innovator, and although he has been deeply influenced by others. Now Smollett was always distinctly himself, even when he was consciously following Le Sage. No man can confound his style with any other, and as Sainte-Beuve has said, it is no small thing to have a style of your own. His presentment of action and character is always done after a fashion which is his and not another man's. Even when he feels other influences he assimilates them. Attempts are sometimes made to rank men of letters, in the Madagascar fashion, into "honours" first, second, third, and so forth to the twentieth. These arrangements look precise, but on the whole they are a trifle barbarous. There are in the main only two divisions in the business of writing: the men who are themselves form one, and the men who are the echoes of somebody else form the other. In the first class there are gradations of merit, but its members are separated by a wide gulf, over which there is no passing, from the second order. Smollett was very distinctly on the right side of the gulf.

THE END.

INDEX.

———◆———

11

BIBLIOGRAPHY.

JOHN P. ANDERSON

(British Museum).

I. WORKS.

The Miscellaneous Works of Tobias Smollett. With a short account of the author [and frontispieces by Rowlandson]. 6 vols. Edinburgh, 1790, 8vo.
    Reprinted with the same plates, Edinburgh, 1809, in 5 vols., 8vo.

The Miscellaneous Works of T. S., with Memoirs of his Life and Writings, by R. Anderson. 6 vols. London, 1796, 8vo.
——Another edition. 6 vols. 1806, 8vo.
——Another edition. 6 vols. Edinburgh, 1811, 8vo.
——Fifth edition, with portrait of Smollett. 6 vols. Edinburgh, 1817, 8vo.

The Miscellaneous Works of T. S. Sixth edition. 6 vols. Edinburgh, 1820, 8vo.
——Another edition. 12 vols. London, 1824, 12mo.

The Works of T. S., with memoirs of his life, to which is prefixed a view of the commencement and progress of romance, by J. Moore. 8 vols. London, 1797, 8vo.
——Another edition, edited by J. P. Browne. 8 vols. London, 1872, 8vo.

The Miscellaneous Works of T. S., complete in one volume, with memoir of the author, by Thomas Roscoe. London, 1841, 8vo.

The Miscellaneous Works of T. S. Another edition, illustrated by George Cruikshank. London, 1845, 8vo.

The Works of T. S., carefully selected and edited from the best authorities, with numerous original historical notes and a life of the author, by David Herbert. Edinburgh, 1870 [1869], 8vo.

II. POETICAL WORKS.

The Poetical Work of Tobias Smollett, to which is prefixed the life of the author (*Anderson's Poets of Great Britain*, vol. x.). Edinburgh, 1794, 8vo.

The Poetical Works of T. S., collated with the best editions, by Thomas Park (*Works of the British Poets*, vol. xli.). London, 1808, 16mo.

The Poems of T. S., with a life by Mr. Chalmers (*Works of the English Poets*, vol. xv.). London, 1810, 8vo.

Select Poems of T. S., with a life of the Author (*Works of the British Poets*, vol. xxxiii). Boston [U.S.], 1822, 12mo.

The Poems of T. S. The life by S. W. Singer (*British Poets*, vol. lxvi). Chiswick, 1822, 12mo.

The Poetical Works of Oliver Goldsmith, Tobias Smollett, etc. Illustrated by John Gilbert. (*Routledge's British Poets.*) London, 1853, 8vo.

The Poetical Works of Johnson, Parnell, Gray, and Smollett. With memoirs, critical dissertations, and explanatory notes, by the Rev. George Gilfillan. Edinburgh, 1855, 8vo.

The Poetical Works of Johnson, Parnell, Gray, and Smollett. Another edition. The text edited by C. C. Clarke. London [1878], 8vo.

The Poetical Works of Oliver Goldsmith, Tobias Smollett, Samuel Johnson, and William Shenstone, with biographical notices and notes. London [1881], 8vo.

III. SELECTIONS.

The Beauties of the Magazines, consisting of essays, moral tales, etc., by Colman, Goldsmith, Murphy, Smollett, etc. 2 vols. London, 1772, 12mo.

——Another edition. 2 vols. London, 1775, 8vo.

Plays and Poems written by T. S., with memoirs of the life and writings of the author. London, 1777, 8vo.

——Another edition. 1784, 8vo.

The Novels of Tobias Smollett, to which is prefixed, a memoir of the life of the author, by Sir Walter Scott. (*Novelists' Library*, vols. ii.; iii.) 2 vols. London, 1821, 8vo.

Illustrations of Smollett, Fielding, and Goldsmith, in a series of forty-one plates, designed and engraved by George Cruikshank. Accompanied by descriptive extracts. London, 1832, 8vo.

The Beauties of Smollett, consisting of selections from his prose and poetry, by A. Howard. London [1834], 12mo.

IV. SINGLE WORKS.

Advice; a Satire [in verse, by T. S.]. London, 1746, fol.

Reproof; a Satire [in verse]. The Sequel to Advice. London, 1747, fol.

Advice and Reproof; two Satires first published in the year 1746 and 1747. London, 1748, 4to.
——Another edition (*British Satirist*). Glasgow, 1826, 12mo.

The Adventures of Roderick Random. 2 vols. London, 1748, 12mo.
——Third edition. 2 vols. London, 1750, 12mo.
——Seventh edition. 2 vols. London, 1766, 12mo.
——Eighth edition. 2 vols. London, 1770, 12mo.
——Tenth edition. 2 vols. London, 1778, 8vo.
——Another edition. 2 vols. London, 1780, 12mo.
——Twelfth edition. 2 vols. London, 1784, 8vo.
——Another edition, abridged by R. Lewis. Dublin, 1791, 12mo.
——Another edition, with the life of the author. 2 vols. London [1793], 12mo.
Vols. viii. and ix. of a series entitled "Cooke's edition of Select British Novels."
——Another edition (*Walker's Classics*). London, 1815, 24mo.
——Another edition, with illustrations by George Cruikshank. (Roscoe's *Novelist's Library*, vol. ii.) London, 1831, 12mo.
——Another edition. (*Tauchnitz Collection of British Authors*, vol. lxxxviii.) Leipzig, 1845, 16mo.
——Another edition. With a memoir of the author [by G. H. T. —*i.e.*, G. H. Townsend]. London, 1857, 8vo.
——Another edition, illustrated by George Cruikshank. London, 1836, 12mo.

The Adventures of Roderick Random. Another edition. London [1867], 8vo.
One of a series, entitled "Routledge's Railway Library."

The Regicide: or, James the First of Scotland. A Tragedy, by the author of Roderick Random. London, 1749, 8vo.

The Adventures of Peregrine Pickle. In which are included, Memoirs of a Lady of Quality. 4 vols. London, 1751, 12mo.
——Second edition. London, 1751, 12mo.
——Third edition. 4 vols. London, 1765, 12mo.
——Fourth edition. 4 vols. London, 1769, 12mo.
——Fifth edition. 4 vols. London, 1773, 12mo.
——Another edition. 4 vols. London, 1781, 8vo.
The pagination is continuous throughout the 4 vols.
——Seventh edition. 4 vols. London, 1784, 12mo.
——Cooke's edition. 4 vols. London [1794], 12mo.
One of a series entitled "Cooke's edition of Select British Novels."
——Another edition. With plates by Rowlandson. 4 vols. Edinburgh, 1805, 8vo.
——Another edition. 2 vols. London, 1815, 12mo.
Each volume has an engraved title-page and frontispiece. This forms part of "Walker's British Classics."
——Another edition, with illustrations by George Cruikshank. (Roscoe's *Novelist's Library*, vols. iii., iv.) 2 vols. London, 1831, 12mo.
——Another edition. With illustrations by Phiz. London, 1857, 8vo.

The Adventures of Peregrine Pickle. Another edition. 2 vols. London, 1882, 8vo.
One of "Routledge's Sixpenny Novels."
——Another edition. London, 1882, 8vo.

Essay on the external use of Water, with particular remarks on the mineral waters of Bath. London, 1752, 4to.

A Faithful Narrative of the base and inhuman arts that were lately practised upon the brain of Habbakkuk Hilding [*i.e.*, Henry Fielding], Justice, Dealer, and Chapman. By Drawcansir Alexander [*i.e.* Tobias Smollett]. London, 1752, 8vo.

The Adventures of Ferdinand, Count Fathom. [By T. S.] 2 vols. London, 1753, 12mo.
——Second edition. 2 vols. London, 1771, 12mo.
——Another edition. 2 vols. London, 1780, 12mo.
——Another edition. 2 vols. London, 1782, 8vo.
The pagination is continuous throughout the 2 vols.
——Another edition. London [1795], 12mo.
One of a series, entitled "Cooke's edition of Select British Novels."

A Compendium of Authentic and Entertaining Voyages digested in a Chronological Series, etc. [Edited by T. Smollett.] 7 vols. London, 1756, 12mo.
——Second edition. 7 vols. London, 1766, 12mo.

The Reprisal : or, the Tars of Old England. A Comedy [by T. S.] of two acts, as performed at the Theatre Royal in Drury Lane. London, 1757, 8vo.

A Compleat History of England, deduced from the descent of Julius Cæsar to the Treaty of Aix-la-Chapelle, 1748, containing the transactions of one thousand eight hundred and three years. 4 vols. London, 1757-58, 4to.
——Second edition. 11 vols. London, 1758-60, 8vo.
——Continuation of the Complete History of England. 5 vols. London, 1763-65, 8vo.
——The History of England from the Revolution to the death of George the Second. (Designed as a continuation of Mr. Hume's History.) A new edition. 5 vols. London, 1789, 8vo.
Numerous subsequent editions.

The Adventures of Sir Launcelot Greaves, by the author of Roderick Random. 2 vols. London, 1762, 12mo.
Originally appeared in the *British Magazine* for 1760-61, when the author was in prison for a libel in the *Critical Review* on Admiral Knowles.
——Another edition. 2 vols. London, 1774, 12mo.
——Another edition. 2 vols. London, 1780, 12mo.
——Another edition. 2 vols. London, 1782, 8vo.
The pagination is continuous throughout the 2 vols.
——Another edition. 2 vols. London, 1783, 12mo.
——Another edition. 2 vols. London, 1793, 12mo.
——Another edition. London, 1810, 24mo.
There is also an engraved title-page dated 1809.
——Another edition, with illustrations by George Cruikshank. (Roscoe's *Novelist's Library*, vol. x.) London, 1832, 12mo.

The Present State of all Nations. Containing a geographical, natural, commercial, and political history of all the countries in the known world. 8 vols. London, 1764, 8vo.

——Another edition. 8 vols. London, 1768-9, 8vo.

Travels through France and Italy, etc. 2 vols. London, 1766, 8vo.

The British Museum possesses a copy with MS. notes by the author.

——Second edition. 2 vols. Dublin, 1772, 12mo.

——Another edition. 2 vols. London, 1778, 12mo.

The History and Adventures of an Atom. By Nathaniel Peacock [*i.e.*, Tobias Smollett]. 2 vols. London, 1749 [1769], 12mo.

——Another edition. 2 vols. London, 1769, 12mo.

——Tenth edition. 2 vols. London, 1778, 12mo.

——Another edition. 2 vols. Edinburgh, 1784, 12mo.

——Another edition. 2 vols. London, 1786, 8vo.

The pagination is continuous throughout the 2 vols.

The Expedition of Humphry Clinker, by the author of Roderick Random. 3 vols. London, 1671 [1771], 12mo.

——Second edition. 3 vols. London, 1772, 12mo.

——Another edition. 2 vols. Edinburgh, 1788, 12mo.

——Fourth edition. 3 vols. London, 1792, 12mo.

——Another edition. 2 vols. London [1794], 12mo.

One of a series, entitled "Cooke's edition of Select British Novels."

——Another edition. 2 vols. London, 1805, 8vo.

The Expedition of Humphry Clinker. Another edition. London, 1808, 12mo.

With a second and engraved title-page.

——Another edition. (*British Novelists*, vols. xxx., xxxi.) 2 vols. London, 1810, 12mo.

——Another edition. London. 1815, 24mo.

——Another edition. With illustrations by George Cruikshank. (Roscoe's *Novelist's Library*, vol. 1.) London, 1831, 12mo.

——Another edition. (*Tauchnitz Collection*, vol. xcii.) Leipzig, 1846, 16mo.

——Another edition. With illustrations by Phiz [*i.e.*, H. K. Browne]. London, 1857, 8vo.

——Another edition. London, 1882, 8vo.

Ode to Independence. With notes and observations. Glasgow, 1773, 4to.

——Another edition. London, 1774, 4to.

——Another edition. Glasgow [1800], 12mo.

V. TRANSLATIONS.

The Adventures of Gil Blas of Santillane. A new translation [by T. S.] from the best French edition. 4 vols. London, 1749, 12mo.

——Another edition. 4 vols. London, 1750, 12mo.

——Another edition. 4 vols. London, 1761, 12mo.

——Fourth edition. London, 1773, 12mo.

Other editions:—London, 1780, 24mo, in 8 vols.; London, 1781, 12mo, in 4 vols.; Dublin, 1785, 12mo, in 4 vols.; London, 1789, 12mo, in 4 vols.; London, 1792, in 4 vols.; London [1793], 12mo, in 4 vols.; London, 1797, 12mo, in 4 vols. ; London, 1818, 12mo, in 2 vols. ; London, 1819, 8vo, in 3 vols.; London, 1826, 12mo, in 4 vols. ; London, 1836, 8vo, in 2 vols., illustrated by Gigoux ; London, 1835, 8vo, edited by T. Roscoe, illustrated by G. Cruikshank ; London, 1841, 8vo, illustrated ; London, 1866, 8vo ; London, 1881, 8vo, in 3 vols., preceded by a biographical and critical notice of Lesage, by George Saintsbury, with twelve original etchings by R. de Los Rios.

The History and Adventures of the renowned Don Quixote. Translated from the Spanish of M. de Cervantes Saavedra. To which is prefixed an account of the author's life. By T. S. [Illustrated with twenty-eight plates designed by Hayman.] 2 vols. London, 1755, 4to.

——Second edition. 4 vols. London, 1761, 8vo.

——Fifth edition. 4 vols. London, 1782, 12mo.

——Sixth edition. 4 vols. London, 1792, 12mo.

——Sixth edition corrected. 4 vols. London, 1793, 12mo.

——Another edition. 4 vols. Dublin, 1796, 8vo.

——Another edition. 5 vols. London [1799], 12mo.

——Another edition, abridged [from Smollett's translation]. Halifax, 1839, 16mo.

The Works of M. de Voltaire. Translated from the French. With notes, historical and critical. [With portraits and frontispieces.] By Dr. Smollet and others. 38 vols. London, 1761-1774, 12mo.

All the volumes, with the exception of the first, bear the name of Dr. T. Francklin in addition to that of Dr. Smollett on the title-page.

——A new edition. London, 1778, etc., 12mo.

The Adventures of Telemachus, the son of Ulysses. Translated from the French by T. S. 2 vols. London, 1776, 12mo.

——Another edition. 2 vols. Dublin, 1793, 12mo.

VI. MISCELLANEOUS.

The Modern Part of an Universal History, from the earliest account of Time. Compiled from original writers by the authors of the Ancient Part. 44 vols. London, 1759-66, 8vo.

Smollett assisted in the compilation of this work, and is supposed, among other articles, to have contributed the *Histories of France, Italy, and Germany.*

The Tears of Scotland. Written in the year 1746.

This Ode was first printed without the author's name in " A Collection of the most esteemed Pieces of Poetry that have appeared for several years : with variety of originals, by the late Moses Mendez." London, 1767, 12mo.

The Critical Review ; or, Annals of Literature. By a Society of Gentlemen. [Edited by T. Smollett.] London, 1756, etc., 8vo.

The British Magazine, or Monthly Repository for Gentlemen and Ladies. [Edited by T. Smollett, assisted by Oliver Goldsmith.] 8 vols. London [1760-67], 8vo.

The Briton. [Edited by T. S.] London (1762-63), fol.

VII. APPENDIX.

BIOGRAPHY, CRITICISM, ETC.

Anderson, Robert.—The Life of Tobias Smollett, with critical observations on his works. London, 1796, 8vo.

Anderson, Robert.—The Life of Tobias Smollett. Second edition. Edinburgh, 1800. 8vo.
——Fourth edition. Edinburgh, 1803, 8vo.
——Fifth edition. Edinburgh, 1806, 8vo.

Anderson, William.—The Scottish Nation; or, the surnames, families, literature, honours, and biographical history of the people of Scotland. 3 vols. Edinburgh, 1863, 8vo.
Tobias Smollett, with portrait, vol. iii., pp. 483-485.

British Plutarch.—The British Plutarch, containing the Lives of the most eminent Statesmen, etc. Third edition. 8 vols. London, 1791, 8vo.
Life of Dr. Tobias Smollett, vol. viii.,.pp. 117-128.

Carlyle, Rev. Dr. Alexander.—Autobiography of the Rev. Dr. A. Carlyle. Edinburgh, 1860, 8vo.
References to T. S. in chaps. iv., vii., and ix.

Cary, Henry Francis.—Lives of the English Poets from Johnson to Kirke White. London, 1846, 8vo.
Tobias Smollett, pp. 119-146.

Cervantes Saavedra, M. de.—Remarks on the proposals lately published [by T. S.] for a new translation of Don Quixote, etc. London, 1755, 8vo.

Chambers, Robert. — Favourite Authors. Smollett : his life and a selection from his writings. London, 1867, 8vo.
——A Biographical Dictionary of eminent Scotsmen. New edition, revised by the Rev. T. Thomson. London, 1870, 8vo.
Tobias Smollett, vol. iii., pp. 380-385.

Chambers Robert—Traditions of Edinburgh. New edition. London, 1869, 8vo.
Smollett's visit to Edinburgh, p. 323.

Comber, Thomas.—A Vindication of the Great Revolution in England in 1688 . . . with a confutation of the character of King James the Second, as misrepresented by the author [Dr. S.] of the complete history of England. London, 1758, 8vo.

Davis, William. — A Second Journey round the Library of a Bibliomaniac, etc. London, 1825, 8vo.
Key to Smollett's History and Adventures of an Atom, pp. 115-118.

Dibdin, Thomas. — Humphry Clinker : a farce, in two acts, by T. D. London, [1828], 12mo.
In vol. iv. of Cumberland's Minor Theatre.

Encyclopædia Britannica.—Encyclopædia Britannica. Ninth edition. Edinburgh, 1887, 4to.
T. Smollett, by Professor Minto, vol. xxii., pp. 183-185.

Forster, John. — The Life and Times of Oliver Goldsmith. Second edition. 2 vols. London, 1854, 8vo.
References to T. S.

Forsyth, William.—The Novels and Novelists of the Eighteenth Century, etc. London, 1871, 8vo.
Smollett, pp. 278-303.

Frail, Lady.—A Parallel between the Characters of Lady Frail and the Lady of Quality in Peregrine Pickle. In which the facts alledged in both are stated and compared, the character of the heroine set in a true light;

the several other characters examined, etc. London, 1751, 8vo.

Frail, Lady.—An apology for the conduct of a Lady of Quality [*i.e.*, Anne, Viscountess Vane] lately traduc'd under the name of Lady Frail ; wherein her case is fairly stated. In a letter from a person of honour, etc. London, 1751, 8vo.

Grainger, J.—A letter to Tobias Smollett, occasioned by his criticism upon a late translation of Tibullus. London, 1759, 8vo.

Grant, James.—Cassell's Old and New Edinburgh. 3 vols. London, 1882, 4to.
References to Smollett.

Hazlitt, William.—Lectures on the English Comic Writers. London, 1819, 8vo.
T. Smollett, pp. 229-233.

Henderson, Andrew.—A second letter to Dr. Samuel Johnson . . . with an impartial character of Doctor Smollet, etc. London [1775], 8vo.

Hill, J.—The History of a Woman of Quality ; or, the Adventures of Lady Frail [*i.e.*, Anne, Viscountess Vane]. By an impartial hand [J. Hill]. London, 1751, 12mo.

Hillard, George Stillman.—Six Months in Italy. 2 vols. London, 1853, 8vo.
Smollett, vol. ii., pp. 295-298.

Hutton, Laurence. — Literary Landmarks of London. London [1885], 8vo.
Tobias Smollett, pp. 280-282.

Irving J.—Some account of the Family of Smollett of Bonhill ; with a series of letters hitherto unpublished, written by Dr. Tobias Smollett. Dumbarton, 1859, 4to.

Irving, J.—The Book of Dumbartonshire : a history of the county, burghs, parishes, and lands, memoirs of families, and notices of industries carried on in the Lennox District. 3 vols. Edinburgh, 1879 4to.
Family of Smollett of Bonhill, vol. ii., pp. 175-208.

Jeaffreson, J. Cordy. — Novels and Novelists from Elizabeth to Victoria. 2 vols. London, 1858, 8vo.
T. Smollett, vol. i., pp, 148-179.

Masson, David.—British Novelists and their styles ; being a critical sketch of the history of British prose fiction. Cambridge, 1859, 8vo.
Smollett, pp. 104-107 ; Fielding and Smollett, pp. 123-145.

Montagu, Lady M. W. — The Letters and Works of Lady M. W. Montagu. 2 vols. London, 1861, 8vo.
References to T. S.

Nichols, John.—Literary Anecdotes of the Eighteenth Century, etc. 9 vols. London, 1812-1815, 8vo.
Numerous references to T. S.

Nicoll, Henry J.—Landmarks of English Literature. London, 1883, 8vo.
T. Smollett, pp. 222-228.

Notes and Queries. — General Index to Notes and Queries. Five series. London, 1856-1880, 4to.
Numerous references to T. S.

Prophecies.—Wonderful Prophecies ; being a dissertation on the existence, nature, and extent of the prophetic powers in the human mind ; and a remarkable prophecy of Dr. Smollett, just before his death, etc. London, 1795, 8vo.

BIBLIOGRAPHY. ix

Reed, Joseph.—A Sop in the Pan for a physical critick ; in a letter to Dr. Sm*ll*t [*i.e.*, Tobias Smollett] occasion'd by a criticism on a late Mock-Tragedy, call'd Madrigal and Trulletta. By a Halter-maker [*i.e.*, Joseph Reed]. London, 1759, 8vo.

Scott, Sir Walter.—A Memoir of the life of Tobias Smollett. (Prefixed to the Novels of T. S. in the *Novelist's Library*, vols. ii. and iii.) London, 1821, 8vo.

Shebbeare, Dr. John.—The Occasional Critic ; or, the decrees of the Scotch tribunal in the Critical Review rejudged. [By Dr. J. Shebbeare.] [London, 1757], 8vo.

Taine, H. A.—Histoire de la Littérature Anglaise. 4 tom. Paris, 1863-64, 8vo.
Smollett, tom. iii., pp. 318-324.
——History of English Literature. Translated by H. van Laun. New edition. 4 vols. Edinburgh, 1873-74, 8vo.
Smollett, vol. iii., pp. 300-306.

Thackeray, W. M.—The English Humourists of the Eighteenth Century. Second edition. London, 1853, 8vo.
Hogarth, Smollett, and Fielding, pp. 219-268.

Tuckerman, Bayard.—A History of English Prose Fiction from Sir Thomas Malory to George Eliot. New York, 1882, 8vo.
Smollett, pp. 211-217.

Tytler, A. F., Lord Woodhouselee.—Essay on the principles of Translation. Third edition. Edinburgh, 1813, 8vo.
Comparison of the translation of Don Quixote by Motteux with that by Smollett, pp. 281-319.

Vane, Lady.—A letter to the Right Honourable the Lady

V——ss V——, occasioned by the publication of her Memoirs in the "Adventures of Peregrine Pickle." London, 1751, 8vo.

Wershoven, F. J.—Smollett et Lesage. Berlin, 1883, 8vo.

Wilkes, John.—The Correspondence of John Wilkes. 5 vols. London, 1805, 12mo.
Letters of Dr. Smollett to Mr. Wilkes, vol. i., pp. 49-51.

Wilson, Daniel. — Memorials of Edinburgh in the Olden Time. Edinburgh, 1872, 4to.
References to Smollett.
——Reminiscences of Old Edinburgh. 2 vols. Edinburgh, 1878, 8vo.
References to Smollett.

MAGAZINE ARTICLES.

Tobias George Smollett.—Quarterly Review, vol. 103, 1858, pp. 66-108 ; same article, Littell's Living Age, vol. 56, pp. 641-695. — Gentleman's Magazine, by George B. Smith, vol. 14, N.S., 1875, pp. 729-737.
——*at Chelsea.* London Magazine, by T. H. Gibson, vol. 2, 1876, pp. 98-103.
——*at Nice.* Macmillan's Magazine, by W. J. Prowse, vol. 21, 1870, pp. 527-533.
——*Count Fathom.* Monthly Review, vol. 8, 1753, pp. 203-214.
——*History of England.* Monthly Review, vol. 16, 1757, pp. 530-536 ; vol. 18, 1758, pp. 289-305 ; vol. 28, 1763, pp. 249-256, 359-369.—Critical Review, vol. 3, 1757, pp. 449-458, 81-499 ; vol. 5, 1758, pp. 1-17.
——*Inedited Memorials of.* Atlantic Monthly, by W. Sargent, vol. 3, 1859, pp. 693-703.

Smollett, Tobias George.
——*Life and Writings of.* London Magazine, vol. 6, 1822, pp. 327-335 ; same article, Portfolio, vol. 15, fourth series, 1823, pp. 89-105.
——*Memoir of.* Museum of Foreign Literature, vol. 5, p. 209, etc.
——*The Regicide.* Monthly Review, vol. 1, 1749, pp. 72-79.
——*Sterne and Fielding.* Portfolio, vol. 6, N.S., 1811, pp.

Smollett, Tobias George.
412-431. — Gentleman's Magazine, by Charles Cowden Clarke, vol. 8, N.S., 1872, pp. 556-580.
——*Translation of Don Quixote.* Monthly Review, vol. 13, 1755, pp. 196-202.
——*Translation of Voltaire's Works.* Monthly Review, vol. 29, 1763, pp. 273-282.
——*Travels through France and Italy.* Monthly Review, vol. 34, 1766, pp. 419-429.

VIII. CHRONOLOGICAL LIST OF WORKS.